Let Them be Naked

Garner shot 'Naked' at Chateau De La Flocelliere

A Handbook for Surviving the Clothes We Wear

By Jeff Garner
With Randall Fitzgerald

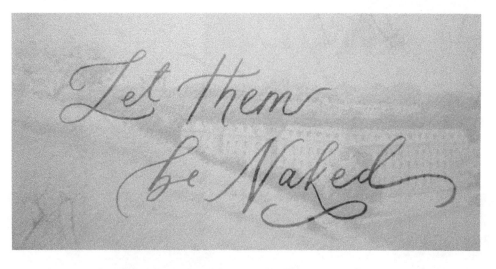

Presented by Suzy Amis Cameron & Inside Out, LLC
Copyright © 2024 by Prophetik, LLC

Front & Back Cover Art painted by Lilly Piper
Cover & layout designed by Jeff Garner
Edited by Ken L. Smith

Library of Congress Cataloging-in-publication Data
Title: Let them be Naked/Prophetik
First Edition, Nashville, TN, IngramSpark 2024
Identifiers: ISBN 979-8-9912358-8-4 (hardcover)
ISBN 979-8-9912358-9-1 (softcover)
ISBN 979-8-99112358-7-7 (ebook)

Manufactured in the United States of America

First Edition

This book may be obtained through your local bookstore or preferred retailer. Retailers may order through Ingram. This book is printed on demand, which reduces environmental impact.

'This book
is dedicated to us~
all of us eight billion
loving souls on earth,
who can heal our planet
and our bodies here
and now '

 ## Dedication

To my mom, Peggy Lynn Garner, & hippie dad, Jim
Wilson, and my sweet angel daughter, Veda Julietta Garner, each of
whom left us too soon

Contents

About the Authors:

Jeff Garner is an award winning Sustainable fashion designer for over 22 years. He is named as one of the top 40 artist in the US by the Smithsonian, with pieces in the Renwick Gallery and the Tennessee State Museum. Jeff uses natural fabrics & plant-based dyes which he grows on his horse farm in Tennessee, and is credited as an expert in sustainable fashion & natural dyes. Jeff has consulted/designed for Whole foods, Quicksilver, Southwest Airlines, Def Leopard, Taylor Swift, Giselle Bundchen, Suzy Amis Cameron, and others. Winning an Emmy in 2019 for the short doc, 'Remastered', in Culture & Art, with his second documentary launching with this book, 'Let them be naked'.

Randall Fitzgerald has been an investigative newspaper and magazine reporter and book author, for over forty years. He has written investigative features for *Reader's Digest*, *The Washington Post*, and *The Wall Street Journal*. Randall is also a NY Times best selling author, with titles such as: 'the *Hundred Year Lie*' & '*Healthy Beauty.*'

INTRODUCTION: When Convenience Spawns Complacency

> "Our lives begin to end the day we become silent about things that matter."
> ---Martin Luther King, Jr.

Let me begin by acknowledging that I am not a seasoned writer (*often I make up my own words),* but rather, a peculiar fashion designer/renaissance artist, with a penchant for long hair and hemp clothing. I made the bold decision to pursue my dream and artistic vision against all odds and certain family members. Let's just say I drove cross-country in my royal blue, topless jeep wrangler to Malibu away from a full ride scholarship to West Point Academy. To carve my niches in the industry, I had to chart a distinct course…one that my resilient Tennessee horse farm mentality took in full gallop. So, off I ventured into a realm where I aimed to craft everything from plants in a world of oil. My own daughter even called me the 'Lorax.'

My aversion to creating art forms that could harm others has been my guiding principle. Despite the sometimes laughter and derision, with labels like 'hippie' 'surfer' thrown my way, I emerged 22 years later, ready to share the genuine and unfiltered truths that I've collected during my unique journey. A sense of public responsibility compels me to share what I've learned, especially considering the losses that I've endured, due to toxins, which I believe infiltrate our bodies through the clothes we choose to wear, simply by the contact of our own skin.

I enlisted the expertise of investigative journalist Randall Fitzgerald, author of '*The One Hundred Year Lie*,' to help compile data from extensive research for this book. We also conducted our own research to complement my narrative and demonstrate that I am not just some isolated forest-ocean-cabin-hippie voice in this industry. I personally have invested 22 years in this mission, research, and design solutions.

I will give a quick synopsis of my career. I started as a young lad in TN, in the Smokey mountains, with my grandmother, Lola, who taught me to sew along with my mother. Growing up with long hair on a horse farm in TN, most of my friends were artists, as we all accepted each other. Naturally, my band friends asked me to dress them. I loved the idea of matching the visual aesthetic with the audible, as most of my music friends read sheet music, and I read colors and fits. Fast forward to my first invitation to show my collection in London. I asked my buddy Phil Collen from Def Leopard, if he would play the catwalk, and to my surprise he said yes. He then asked what I would like the lead out song to be and I said "brown sugar" lol. I am still bad with names to this day. We rocked that catwalk with Cara Delevingne being my lead muse model..we had a special bond then, both innocent freshman in this crazy world of fashion. So began my catwalk career, with the intention to show beautiful dresses dyed with plants and made of natural fabrics. I naively thought the industry would say ok here's a great example now lets do it! But being a stubborn horse farm boy I just kept riding harder.

I built collections with no funding…selling band tees on the side… sourcing fabric even from curtains to dye and create into a dress. I made magic out of remnants to keep showing. I have produced over 100 catwalk shows & 16 years of designing 30-42 pieces per collection. I have shown at London Fashion Week, Milan Fashion week, NYC fashion week, Paris Fashion week, Vancouver Fashion week, Shanghai Fashion week, and more. I have produced specialty shows for countries and US embassies in Lisbon, Monaco, Smithsonian Museum in DC, Edinburgh Castle in Scotland and many others.

A harsh reality is that the truth about what we wear has been obscured and manipulated for profit. As you read what follows, be prepared to be flabbergaskily shocked (and yes, I made up that word) You will probably wonder why this information hasn't been more widely shared and commonly known. Let me assure you that I have no hidden motives or vested interests in presenting this information. I have no monetary incentive. My friends try to buy things from me all the time, and, to their dismay, I say: "Sorry I don't have time." If anything, I am investing more than I can gain financially to bring everything to the proverbial 'table'.

Despite my preference for solitude in my cedar cabin in the forest, I am making myself publicly vulnerable in these pages, because I am driven by a concern for the future of humanity and for improving people's quality and longevity of life.

Someone once said the universe isn't short on wake-up calls, and we're just too quick to hit our snooze buttons. My hippie dad, Jim, always told me: *"Wherever you are is the entry point."* As most creative dreamers, I was born with a calling, yet it ignited when my three-year-old daughter, Veda, lost her precious life due to a heart condition triggered in the womb, by her mother's poisoning from exposure to toxic crop-dusting chemicals from her family's business.

This wake-up amplified and grew more urgent when my own mother, Peggy, died later from breast cancer at the age of 70. It was mainly caused by the nylon-polyester, carcinogenic bras that she wore most of her life. Unknowingly to her, they had been doused with toxic synthetic chemicals during manufacturing.

As you might imagine, as a result of these knee-buckling experiences, spreading a message about the origins of toxins, their hidden dangers to human health and their threat to our planet's entire environment, has become quite a personal quest. I know too much to allow more people to suffer due to my silence. Plus, I have always been a rebellious spirit.

Often, I've considered myself an Aesthete, as a lone individual confronted by nature. Aesthetes (the writer Oscar Wilde being a good example) believed that life must be lived intensely, through an ideal of beauty, addressing the deficiencies of modern fashion and rejecting contemporary dress. They looked to past groups of progressive artists and intellectuals. The aesthetes sought a return to the old methods of clothing production, using natural dyes, hand looms, and hand worked details, because the modern fashion emerging from the Industrial Revolution offended both taste and reason with poor quality, mass-produced clothing that harmed the individual wearer and the environment.

Everyone should treat the topic of toxins in clothes personally, even if you have not yet suffered personal tragedy, as I have. The reason simply: one of the biggest and largest unrecognised contributors to bioaccumulation of toxins comes through our skin into our bloodstream, from direct contact with the clothing we choose to wear everyday, all day long.

Shocking.. After all, can we not depend on assurances from clothing manufacturers and government regulatory agencies that everything we place on our skin is guaranteed to be safe? Through our documentary & my experience as a designer I have discovered, in reality, it is quite the opposite. Here is where complacency and a creeping naiveté has set in, from our simply choosing to push our snooze buttons. Trust has been misplaced, our best intentions undermined, as science evidence presented in this book and its companion documentary.

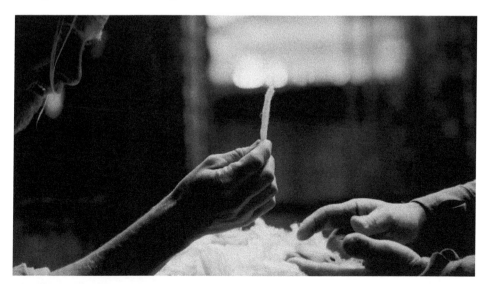

⚜ Exposing the Big Dirty Secret

When compared to how our ancestors lived, it's clear that most of us in highly industrialised countries exist in comparative comfort, as shaped and defined by the availability of everyday conveniences. I am seventh-generation Cherokee, obviously an American mutt of English descent, but also descended from Chief Whooping Crane (Kunnochatutloh), from the North Carolina/Tennessee border. One of the 'sayings' from his tribe is *"what you do today will affect seven generations later."* Seven is a sacred number and reflective in the honour given to seven generations ahead. It's time to address the diseases killing our nation through industrialised convenience. We have wide access to relatively cheap fast food, just as we benefit from the availability of fast fashion clothing, which remains largely at price points set three decades ago.

Just like cooking, 'fast' fashion uses cheap, synthetic chemical ingredients, many of them being toxic, in every stage of the manufacturing and distribution, without accountability to what those cheap ingredients do to the human body.

Yet the price consumers pay for this cheapness comes with hidden costs to human, animal, and environmental health. It's a dirty secret that's been in garments since the end of World War II, when synthetics emerged to dominate fashion and commerce. We ran out of silk parachutes for the war and created nylon to replace silk, but never studied the synergy of effect of what happens when you put this polymer, made from adipic acid and hexamethylene diamine, on the body. The clothing industry still uses industrial grade toxic chemicals that have been outlawed in our food production. So why are they in our clothes?

We have taken clothing conveniences for granted, often in the mistaken belief that their benefits—and their dangers—have, by now, been clearly identified and widely publicised. Big mistake! We are guilty of collective complacency.

My own experience gives testament to how lives can be disrupted and lives can be lost by taking the safety of life's essentials and life's conveniences for granted. Not only did I lose my daughter and my mother, but my hippie dad, Jim, also died of cancer, at age 73, probably from contact with lifestyle-toxins. I know of countless others who have suffered the consequences by believing the myth that some unknown entity has their best interest at heart, and would never produce a textile or garment that could hurt another. For example, Nylon is a thermoplastic that off-gases nitrous oxide made of caustic soda, chloroform, and carcinogenic formaldehyde. I don't think ladies would replace their silk stockings with nylon stockings knowing this!

Bear in mind that it's not just the cheap, 'fast' convenience clothing in our throwaway culture that should alarm us. As an industry veteran, I know firsthand that toxins aren't restricted to what's cheap and mass produced. Toxins show up regularly in high fashion, embedded into the priciest of garments. They may be shimmering with elegance, but many contain toxic residues as a shameful legacy to hide. Oh! The places we will go!

Empowering You with Choice

Average consumers are understandably confused as a result of how fashion and clothing information is generated and communicated and who controls the flow of 'education' and influence. The dimensions between making a profit and promoting sustainable, healthy clothing has been blurred, resulting in a massive amount of misfortune. Some culprits stand out, some of whom will be identified.

What these toxins lurking in clothing do to your body –and to the bodies of those you care about and who depend on you for guidance-- should give us all a long pause of serious reflection and concern. It's subject which affects each of us, whether we realise it or not, or whether we want to acknowledge it or not. Do men really know that wearing polyester boxers are linked to impotence and low sperm count? Do women know that bras are linked to breast cancer more so than cigarettes to lung cancer? Only took 30 years to get the proof out!

We have many questions to raise and to answer for you. What problems do the cheap, toxic ingredients that manufacturers use really inflict upon the human body? Do they off-gas during wear and off-load during washing with impacts on the environment? What kinds of diseases result that may impact humans and wildlife? What happens when those clothing chemicals mix with other convenience of life chemicals to cause synergies? Ever seen your underarm on your t-shirt change colour due to the aluminium in your deodorant mixed with the heavy metals in the t-shirt dye? How much of what should be important to us does science not yet know or isn't yet telling us?

While I do support creative commerce and free markets to benefit consumers, I don't do so automatically and unconditionally, at the price of human health and the preservation of human life. There can, and must, be a peaceful coexistence. The health perils are real and growing, as you will discover in these pages, but the solutions are also readily available and eminently doable, if you have the will to do it, and you exercise the power of choice.

As a Knight of the Order of St. George, a confraternity of men and women with a charitable mission of compassion and chivalry, I took an Oath to protect those who cannot protect themselves. This has become my life's mission: to reveal the identity of the toxins in our fabrics and dyes, in ways that enable all consumers to make educated decisions about what's safe to place next to skin. My intent and ultimate goal has been to help resuscitate our authority for choice.

'Women of the Crown' Catwalk at Edinburgh Castle, Scotland

Consider the information detailed in this book and its *Let Them Be Naked* companion documentary to be a clarion call to help you to help us to shatter our complacency with mindful and impassioned action. As in all industries unless the consumer demands it the shift will not happen as we all know the motivation is mostly always profit in society today.

Collective Consciousness Shifts Begin with Individual Acts

"There needs to be a shift in consciousness; there needs to be an absolute wake-up call before society can actually make the kind of incredibly significant changes that need to happen."--**Annie Lennox**

"Humankind has not woven the web of life. We are but one thread within it. Whatever we do to the web, we do to ourselves. All things are bound together. All things connect."

- **Chief Seattle, Duwamish**

"Friend do it this way-that is, whatever you do in life, do the very best you can with both your heart and minds. And if you do it that way, the Power of the Universe will come to your assistance, if you heart and mind are in Unity. When one sits in the Hoop Of The People, one must be responsible because All of Creation is related. And the Hurt of one is the hurt of all. And the honour of one is the honour of all. And whatever we do effects everything in the universe. If you do it that way-that is, if you truly join your heart and mind as One-whatever you ask for, that is the Way it's Going to be."

- Lakota Instructions for Living passed down from **White Buffalo Calf Woman**

Interviewing Model Activist
Quannah Chasinghorse

Chapter I: Lest We Forget Our Clothing Origins

Natural Sources of Fabric Were Non-Toxic

ꟽy hippie dad, Jim, taught me a lot in life. One of the wisdoms that resonates the most, after I had some recourse of a poor decision I made. He said, *"You choose suffering, because you have more to learn."*

Jeff's Indigo Plant dye vat in TN

Prophetik Silk Chiffon/Madeira Lace Gown indigo plant dyed in Florence, Italy

I began my study of fashion history in Florence, Italy at the age of 19. I was the long-haired, vagabond cafe artist, found sitting on the steps of the Duomo with chalked fingers and leather sketchpad in hand. I learned the art of plant dyes in Florence, being the birthplace of the Renaissance, with the vibrancy of the freedom of artists not controlled by the money of the catholic church…art for art's sake!

ⅅy favourite story was the one of Michelangelo Simoni when
he took on what no other would touch…a large, beautiful piece of
marble called "ll Gigante" abandoned in the Santa Maria del Fiore
church courtyard that had one dark vein running through it. One who
even chipped near that vein would crack the entire marble. When asked
what he would sculpt out of the marble, he replied…*"I am only freeing
what is inside."* You can see the dark vein running up the back of the
leg. This piece became what most of the world knows as
Michelangelo's The David!

When archaeologists excavated a cemetery in northwest China, near the modern city of Turfan, they were astonished to find impeccably preserved items of 3,200-year-old clothing, including a remarkable pair of stylish and durable trousers with multiple advanced design features.

An international team of textile archaeologists and fashion designers, brought in to study the weaving methods used on the trousers, identified several weaving techniques, two of them unique to these trousers. One was a twill weave used to connect the various parts of the trousers that had been crafted from yarn made of coarse sheep's wool.

This twill weave produced a diagonal decorative pattern of parallel ribs, giving the wearer increased mobility, because the fabric became more elastic. This was perfectly suited for the comfort and movement needs of someone who spent a lot of time riding horses bareback, as *The Turfan Man* (the name this wearer was given) apparently did daily.[1]

Added textile archaeologist Karine Gromer of Vienna's Natural History Museum: "It's like the Rolls-Royce of trousers."[2]

Today, I make my riding pants out of hemp, as it is the strongest tensile strength of any other fabric thus would last forever unless your horse throws you into a barbed wire fence!

---

[1] "The world's oldest pants stitched together cultures from across Asia." ScienceNews. February 18, 2022. M. Wagner ET AL/Archaeological Research in Asia 2022

[2] "Ancient fashion: 3,200-year old pants on Chinese mummy are like modern-day jeans." BigThink. September 5, 2023.

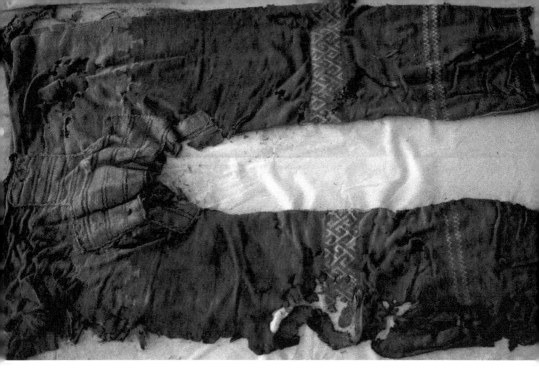

If we compare the Turfan Man's ancient natural trousers to a pair of synthetic-laden Jeans produced today, we find that both may be durable, stylish and comfortable, but as you can imagine, no synthetic chemicals were added to Turfan Man's wardrobe. Trousers comparable to Turfan Man's manufactured today (*Ironically, Turfan now is a industry plant city producing chemicals, textiles, and coal mines.*) contain a devilish brew of toxic chemicals—from cancer-causing azo dyes and formaldehyde to residues of pesticides and finishing agents—all with the potential to harm human health.

Which trousers would you prefer your loved ones to wear?

As this handbook will show, what these Turfan Man trousers illustrate for us today is that millennia ago, our ancestors were producing toxin-free, ecologically friendly and sustainable clothing that not only stood the test of time, but equals modern clothing in its durability and comfort, while exceeding modern toxin-laden clothing in health and safety standards.

Our Natural Clothing Heritage

We humans lived a mostly hairy and naked existence, until evolution resulted in our ancestors losing a great percentage of their body hair, about 300,000 or more years ago, according to evolutionary biologists. That hair loss helped create the need for garments, mostly made from matted leaves and grass, and later, from animal hides, to protect against cold temperatures and other vagaries of Nature.

Sewing needles made of ivory and bone have been carbon-dated to between 30,000 and 40,000 B.C., so that gives us a clue about the timeline origins of what we call the home garment industry.[3]

An urge for self-expression and creativity began to supplement practical clothing needs with body ornamentation, somewhere around 41,000 B.C., in both Africa and Europe. Shells, teeth, ivory and stone provided the materials for beads and jewelry adornments, and, though not much clothing survives from that period, we can be confident that garment styles also became statements conferring identity and social status.[4]

Because linen was found by archaeologists in a cave in the Caucasus mountains of southern Russia, it's believed that flax may have been the first textile to be produced for clothing, about 36,000 years ago, Within the past 10,000 years, along with the widespread development of agricultural practices, the natural fibres (silk, wool,

[3] "Origin of Clothing Lice Indicates Early Clothing Use by Anatomically Modern Humans in Africa." Toups MA. Et al. *Molecular Biology and Evolution.* 2011 January.

[4] "Archaeologists Home in on Body Ornament Origins." Kate Wong. *Scientific American.* June 5, 2001.

cotton, flax, and hemp) all emerged in a range of cultures for fashioning into textile fabrics.[5]

In the 7th century BC, the oldest recorded use of fibre comes with the invention of flax and wool fabric, as shown by archaeological excavations in the Swiss lake region. Whereas in India and Eastern Africa the growing and weaving of cotton into cloth goes back to 5000 BC, the development of spin silk methods got initiated in China about 2640 BC, and in Egypt, the art of spinning and weaving linen can be traced to at least 3400 BC.[6]

By the time we get to the 18th century, at least in North America, cotton had emerged as the primary fibre for clothing, a result of the invention of the cotton gin in 1793, to sort cotton seed from cotton fibre. In many ways the establishment of cotton mills before the U.S. Civil War marked the initiation of an Industrial Revolution in America.[7]

We have no indication from the historical record that cotton, linen, and other natural fibre clothes were ever considered a direct danger to human health. It's difficult to imagine an ancient Roman pointing to his toga and warning, "this thing could be the death of me!" No one could have predicted that the future of clothing would involve dosing them with synthetic chemicals sufficient to place human health and planetary health in peril.

[5] Alliance for European Flax-Linen & Hemp. https://allianceflaxlinenhemp.eu/en/all-about-european-linen/flax-linen-in-history

[6] "The Textile Revolution: Transforming the Fabric." Textile School. Oct 4, 2023. https://www.textileschool.com/182/history-of-textiles-ancient-to-modern-fashion-history/

[7] "History of the American Textile Industry." Nanjiba Nur. *Textile Focus*. August 11, 2022.

Oscar Wilde's half-sisters 'on fire'

 Until Killer Clothes Do We Part

Irish playwright, poet, and aesthete, **Oscar Wilde,** experienced firsthand, during the late 19th century, how hidden dangers lurking in clothing could result in a shortened life. His two half-sisters, Emily and Mary, both caught fire and burned to death at a Halloween ball in Dublin when their highly flammable dresses brushed against a hot fireplace during a ball room dance.

Ten years later, Oscar Wilde's wife, Constance, founded an organization of London high society women dedicated to safe clothing, called The Rational Dress Society. The group described itself this way in 1881: *"We protest against the introduction of any fashion in dress that either deforms the figure, impedes the movements of the body, or in any way tends to injure the health."*

L' hotel, Paris, Last room of Oscar Wilde

An initial target of The Rational Dress Society was *"perhaps the most restrictive and unsafe item of clothing introduced in the name of fashion during the nineteenth (or any other) century…the corset,"* commented the authors of *Killer Clothes.* *"It squeezed women's bodies and crushed their internal organs, even displacing their ribs, until women could hardly breathe or move without experiencing pain. These virtual straitjackets were worn because many women chose to believe these garments made the feminine form more shapely and desirable to men."* Another fun fact I learned in Florence was that the designer of the corset was Catherine de Medici married from the wealthy banking family of Florence, to the King of France, Henry II, making the corset fashionable in French court.

For someone who once wrote, ***"One should either be a work of Art, or wear a work of Art,"*** Oscar Wilde certainly wasn't distasteful of fashion. In fact, he was one of the most avant-garde flamboyant fashion tastemakers of his century. It was just that he and his wife felt adamant —and with good reason borne of experience-- that the clothes we choose to wear shouldn't present a clear and present danger. We should never be forced to sacrifice our health and our life on the altars of short-sighted convenience or unsafe fashion choices.

A similar health-protective case was made during the same period by German physician **Gustav Jager,** who championed many causes in the name of health, chief among them the wearing of safe, non-toxic clothing. He was one of the first healthy fashion promoters to single out the dangers of aniline dyes, also called coal tar dyes, which in the mid-19th century became the foundation for the world's synthetic dye industry.[8]

Up until the accidental discovery of aniline dyes by a young British chemistry student in 1856, virtually all clothing dyes had come from natural sources (plants, animals, minerals) including most prominently the colour purple from shellfish, which had been the royal colour reserved only for Roman emperors. As more aniline dye colours

---

[8] Textile Research Centre. https://trc-leiden.nl/trc-needles/materials/dyes/aniline

were created and introduced into clothing, the market for the use of natural dyes collapsed in most countries.

Within a decade of the aniline dye's introduction to mainstream clothing, some wearers began reporting painful rashes from skin contact with gloves and stockings coloured by the dyes, the first documented widespread contagion of contact dermatitis. There was even a photographic display at the 1884 International Health Exhibition held in London, under the patronage of Queen Victoria, showing the rashes caused by aniline-dyed clothing.[9]

Fashion has always harboured an unacknowledged dark side, argued Alison Matthews David, Professor of Fashion at Toronto Metropolitan University, who wrote the book, **Fashion Victims.** *"Clothing has been the cause of death, disease and madness throughout*

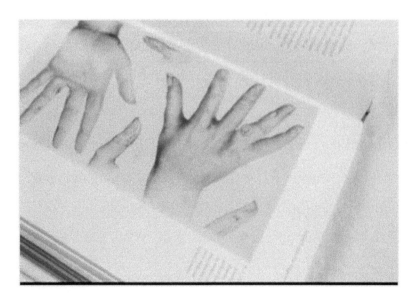

Skin burns from synthetic dyes *'Fashion Victims'*

[9] "Terminology: What Are Aniline Dyes?" The Dreamstress. September 19, 2013. https://thedreamstress.com/2013/09/terminology-what-are-aniline-dyes-or-the-history-of-mauve-and-mauveine/

history, by accident and design. Clothing is designed to protect, shield and comfort us, yet lurking amongst seemingly innocuous garments we find hats laced with mercury, frocks laden with arsenic and literally 'drop-death gorgeous' gowns."

With the introduction of synthetics, both fibres and dyes, into clothing, during the 19th century and accelerating into the 20th, an entire new realm of challenging perils materialised to confront humans, animals, and the global environment. As you will discover in the following chapters, vital information which had previously been hidden or taken for granted—about the clothing chemicals absorbed by our skin that endanger our health---now stands open to naked exposure, no longer easy for any conscientious person to ignore.

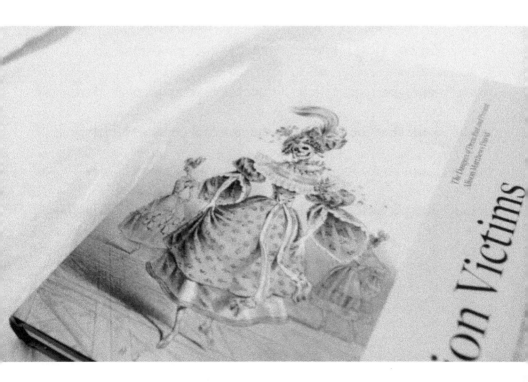

⚜ A Brief Timeline of Synthetic Fibres & Dyes

Aniline Dyes, **1856:** made of a coal-tar byproduct, ranks as the first synthetic organic dye to be discovered and manufactured. Inhalation and dermal exposure to it in sufficient quantities can result in tremors, cardiac arrhythmia, coma or even death.[10]

Azo Dyes, **1875:** German chemical manufacturer Badische Anilinin & Soda-Factory (BASF), began producing this class of synthetic dyes that would eventually be found, in the 20th century, to be carcinogenic to human and aquatic life, at a time when these dyes would account for 70% of all dyes used on clothing.

Rayon, **1891:** A semi-synthetic fibre, a substitute for silk, made from regenerated cellulose (plant fibre) that has been chemically modified, the first commercial production of it began at a factory in France, based on the work of industrial chemist Count Hilarie deCardonnet, known as the father of the rayon industry. Off-gassing from treatment with toxic chemicals during its production can result in neurophysiological effects and other health symptoms.

---

[10] "Synthetic Threads." ScienceHistory.org. Oct. 3, 2016.

Nylon, **1939:** this artificial silk, developed by DuPont Company scientists, and derived from petrochemicals, was introduced in hosiery to the public at the World's Fair, as part of DuPont's Wonder World of Chemistry exhibit. Wearing nylon was found to cause allergic reactions and respiratory issues in some people. It isn't biodegradable and it sheds micro-plastics into the environment. Nylon uses caustic soda, chloroform, sulphuric acid, and formaldehyde during its manufacturing and off gasses Nitrous Oxides and carbon monoxide.[11]

Polyester, **1950:** Made from a combination of petroleum, coal, air and water, DuPont opened a pilot plant in 1950, producing Dacron polyester fibre, though the fibre was first patented by British scientists at the Imperial Chemical Industries in 1928. Chemicals used in the production and processing of polyester, such as xylene & ethylene, were eventually found to be endocrine disrupters and respiratory illness triggers; Antimony trioxide, used as a catalyst in production, may cause cancer in humans.

---

11 "A Timeline of Textile History." Textile Heritage Museum. heritagemuseum.org/textiles-ancient-times-to-modern-day/

Acrylic, **1955:** DuPont Company chemists developed the first acrylic, under the brand name, Orlon, in 1941, but not until the mid-1950's was acrylic manufactured for the marketplace for sweaters, tracksuits, gloves, etc. Designed for convenience, no more hand washing wool sweaters), for with acrylic you can machine wash as they marketed for the stay-at-home moms. Science studies would eventually reveal, that acrylic releases high levels of micro-plastic particles during washing, five times more than polyester/cotton fabric blends.[12]

Spandex, **1958:** brand name Lycra, a stretchable form-fitting fibre, invented by chemist Joseph Shivers at the DuPont Company, it's based on petrochemicals. Decades after widespread introduction into the garment market, science studies discovered that when wearers sweat under a layer of Spandex, chemicals embedded in the fibres can be released into the skin, such as dyes and formaldehyde and polyurethane, which can damage the kidneys, liver and brain. Spandex (now called Lycra or Lycra Spandex) is made of at least 85% of the polymer polyurethane. Spandex is made from several chemicals that are known sensitisers. TDI & MDI (Toluene-2,4-diisocyanate; Methylene

---

[12] "Timeline of Manmade Fibers." TextileSchool. Textileschool.com/351/timeline-of-manmade-fibers/

bisphenyl-4,4-diiisocyanate) are precursors of the polyurethane used to make spandex. TDI proved carcinogenic and can cause severe dermatitis. MDI is also toxic.[13]

***Lyocell*, 1972:** Originally developed by American Enka, semi-synthetic, the transformation of lyocell fibers into fabric and garments can use many or the same harsh, and even toxic, chemicals and processes used in conventional textiles. This is because of two properties of lyocell: it doesn't always accept dyes well, and it has an inherent tendency to fibrillate or "pill". Trademarked as Tencel in 1982, a sub-category of rayon & also trademarked under *Newcell & Seacell.*

13 "Classifications, properties, recent synthesis and applications of azo dyes." Benkhaya S. Et al. Heliyon. 2020 January.   http://latexallergyresources.org/articles/cotton-nylon-spandex-and-allergies#sthash.o8vqAOJa.dpu

Synthetics Are Grossly Energy Intensive

A study done by the Stockholm Environment Institute, on behalf of the BioRegional Development Group, concluded that the **energy used** (and therefore the CO_2 emitted) **to create 1 ton of spun fibre is much higher for synthetics than for hemp or cotton:**

KG of CO2 emissions per ton of spun fiber:			
	crop cultivation	fiber production	TOTAL
polyester USA	0.00	9.52	9.52
cotton, conventional, USA	4.20	1.70	5.90
hemp, conventional	1.90	2.15	4.05
cotton, organic, India	2.00	1.80	3.80
cotton, organic, USA	0.90	1.45	2.35

The table above only gives results for polyester. Other synthetics have more of an impact: **acrylic is 30% more energy intensive in its production than polyester, nylon is even higher than that. Nylon, for example, creates emissions of N2O, which is 300 times more**

damaging than CO2. Because of its long life (120 years) it can reach the upper atmosphere and deplete the layer of stratospheric ozone, which is an important filter of UV radiation. During the 1990s, N2O emissions from a single nylon plant in the UK were thought to have a global warming impact equivalent to more than 3% of the UK's entire CO2 emissions. A study done for the New Zealand Merino Wool Association showed how much less total energy is required for the production of natural fibers than for synthetics.

 ## Design Failures Shadow the Textile Industry

"Textiles are quite literally woven into the fabric of life. The industry that launched the Industrial Revolution has long illustrated some of its most notorious design failures. About one half of the world's wastewater problems are linked to the production of textile goods, and many of the chemicals used to dye and finish fabrics are known to harm human health." –Cradle to Cradle: Remaking the Way We Make Things, by Michael Braungart and William McDonough, 2002.

Jeff's bark dye

⚜ Use of Dangerous Dyes Persist

"Dyes have a long history and constitute an important component in our daily lives. The dye industry began by using natural plant and insect sources, and then rapidly turned to synthetic manufacturing processes. Unfortunately, several of the synthetic dyes, especially azo dyes, have been found to be toxic and mutagenic, and are banned throughout the world. However, because of their low cost and other desirable properties, the use of manufacture of azo dyes continues even today." –"Azo dyes: past, present and the future." Bafna A. Et al. *Environmental Reviews*. 2011 .

Synthetic chemicals birthed in laboratories are designed to kill something, preserve something, clean something or mask the symptoms of something. They will outlive us unless we take action.

Gisele Bundchen wearing Jeff's plant dyed Teal (indigo/marigold) hemp/silk couture gown

Summer Rayne Oaks wearing Garner's
elephant painted hemp/silk cocktail dress

Scottish textiles couture gown by
Garner shot at Camelot

Chapter II: A Clothing Industry Soaked in Oil & Blood

Clothing Toxins are a Fossil Fuel Legacy

"Fashion has an enormous environmental {and health} footprint, from the production process through to the disposal of used and unused clothes. Clothing manufacturing requires a considerable amount of energy and resources, uses toxic fabric dyes and other chemicals that contaminate fresh water, and requires synthetic materials made from fossil fuels." *"Do Clothes Make Us Sick? Fashion, Fibers and Human Health." Plastic Soup Foundation, 2022.*

Garner LFW 'Lady Godiva' Burlington Arcade

Textile Waste Beach near Jakarta in Indonesia from the Documentary

 Textile Chain Manufacturing Processes

More than 15,000 synthetic chemicals are available to use during clothing manufacturing. Multiple chemicals are added at each of these production stages.

Raw Fiber Production

Pretreatment Processes

Textile De-sizing

Removing Hydrophobic Substances

Textile Bleaching

Mercerizing the Textile

Textile Dyeing

Dye Treatment Aftermath

Pattern Printing

Finishing

 ## Out of the Ground, Onto Our Skin

One thing I did not mention in the introduction, regarding my full ride to West Point Academy. It was garnered from the ASVAB (*Armed Services Vocational Aptitude Battery)* testing in High-school, where I scored the highest percentile in the country. Since my grandfather, Cecil Lynn, was the first chemist J. Robert Oppenheimer hired for the Manhattan Project at the Oak Ridge, TN Factory, I was in line for the Nuclear Arms program. Obviously, I wanted to use my mind to help people, so as anyone who loves Sherlock Holmes and critical problem solving would think, why does the industry continue to get away with using these deathly mixes for cheap production. Any tracking of the origins of the global clothing industry and why the industry does not shift to cleaner practices should begin with the German chemical firm, **BASF**, which began in 1865, as a dye manufacturer, and rapidly grew into an international industrial giant.

In 1925, the company merged with several other German chemical companies to become the chemicals conglomerate **IG Farben**, which played a major role in the **economy of Nazi Germany**.

IG Farben used forced and slave labor during the Nazi period and produced the notorious **Zyklon B (hydrogen cyanide)** chemical used in the gas chambers of The Holocaust. At the end of World War II, IG Farben was disbanded, though BASF was reconstituted from the remnants of IG Farben in the early 1950s.

BASF has historically received criticism for its poor environmental record. Most recently, it was ranked the **planet's #2 largest polluter of air and #14 largest polluter of water** in 2020, the most recent year for which data is available, according to the 2022 "Top 100 Polluters Indexes" published by the *University of Massachusetts, Amherst's Political Economy Research Institute.*

Not only that, but the Sweden-based, non-governmental organization, ChemSec, **ranked BASF as one of the world's biggest polluters of people and the environment with the 'forever' PFAS chemicals**, used to make fabrics resistant to stains and water. This class of chemicals has been linked to cancer, thyroid disease, birth defects, autoimmune disease, kidney dysfunction, and other health problems. One would start to digress that BASF would not so easily let go of its market of toxic chemicals. Hence why we have not moved away in clothing production from this co-dependency. *"Societal costs of 'forever chemicals' about $17.5tn across global economy."*[1]

By the late-20th century, most of the world's clothing manufacturers had evolved into a well-oiled production machine, with high efficiency and escalating profits, but at the expense of human and planetary health. It's become the fourth-largest industry in the entire world, with two-thirds of all textile fabrics being synthetic and more than half made from oil-based polyester.[2]

This clothing value chain starts with the oil industry extracting and refining crude oil, and it's using heating and distillation processes that release harmful chemicals into the atmosphere. This becomes the building blocks used by the chemical industry, to produce oil-based polyester (plastic) garments. By the year 2020, polyester accounted for 52 percent of the global fiber market.[3]

At the next stage of this chain, the chemical industry supplies {polyethylene terephthalate} pellets or chips to the textile industry, which converts the pellets into fibers, and into fabrics following. This part of the process incorporates the insertion of a wide selection of dyes and additives into the fibers and fabrics.

---

[1] Tom Perkins. The Guardian. May 12, 2023.

[2] "Analysis of the polyester clothing value chain is needed to identify key intervention points for sustainability." Palacios-Mateo C. Et al. *Environ Sci Eur*. 2021.

[3] "Do Clothes Make Us Sick? Fashion, Fibers and Human Health." Plastic Soup Foundation, 2022.

Next, the clothing manufacturers cut and sew the fabric into garments and make them available to the retail store industry. *"All these steps required significant amounts of energy…the dyeing and finishing step is ranked first in terms of environmental harm, considering the following five impact indicators: climate change, freshwater withdrawal, depletion of resources, ecosystem quality, and human health,"* observed the European Union's Joint Research Centre.[4]

Among the chemicals added to textile fibers during these steps are colorants, flame retardants, and PFAS, which are used for waterproofing. Other chemicals used in textiles include stiffening agents, stabilisers, antibacterial agents, plasticisers, anti-shrinking agents, crease resistant compounds, and a wide range of dyestuffs and pigments. Still more chemicals added to textiles include surfactants (compounds that decrease surface tension), solvents, softeners, acids, preservatives, etc.[5]

*Note about **polyester**: It's only one compound in a class of oil-based chemicals called polymers. Little molecules composing polymers are called monomers, the building blocks of synthetic fibers, while long molecules are known as the polymers. The **monomers are carcinogens** and are the **most toxic and harmful to human health, even at low levels**. These monomeric forms may enter the human body through skin.** Monomers off-gas contaminant chemicals and can remain in*

---

[4] "Environmental Improvement Potential of textiles (IMPRO textiles)." European Commission's Joint Research Centre, 2014.

[5] "Engaging the textile industry as a key sector in saicm. A review of PFAS as a chemical class in the textile sector." Yiliqy AR. Lennett D. 2021.

landfills for decades, without decomposing. So, when you hear these "green" companies talking about recycling polyester garments, after knowing the science presented, do you think it is the best solution for your body?

Microscopic image of polyester fabric showing the oil like fibers

Scientists, who study this supply chain, mince no words about the inherent safety dangers of these mixtures: *"Conventional oil-based polyethylene terephthalate (PET) polyester garments compromise the quality of land, water and air, destroys ecosystem, and endangers human health. Conventional PET creates pollution along its entire value chain—during the production, use and end-of-life phases—and also contributes to the unsustainable depletion of resources,"* concluded three scientists with the Science and Engineering Department of Maastricht University in The Netherlands.[6]

Compounding the problems inherent with oil-based synthetics in textiles—particularly the health consequences, both those consequences revealed and those remaining to be revealed-manufacturers have lubricated the garment supply chain with practices which enhance profits yet continue to multiply problems.

---

[6] "Analysis of the polyester clothing value chain to identify key intervention points for sustainability." Palacios-Mateo C. Et al. *Environ Sci Eur*. 2021.

(Danufacturing Horrors 'Fast Fashion' & 'Nano-Particles"

 A Strategy of Haste Makes Waste

(Dany textile manufacturers and retailers, prominent among them would be Zara, H&M and Primark, embraced a business strategy in the late 1990s, one that continues to the present day, known as *fast-fashion*—though it should really be called disposable waste apparel, or planned obsolescence clothing. It's a monumentally wasteful practice that resembled steroids being injected into the clothing production system, "knocking off" designers like myself that catwalk at fashion week and getting those designs to market cheaply, the following week, creating trend & desire for the latest fashions, using slave labor and toxic ingredients.When someone's song lyrics are copied, their likeness, their voice, or their painting, they are protected, but not in fashion. Fashion has moved away from art, and it has become a business of logo trademarks (such as GUCCI, etc), textile fabrics owned (Lycra, wicker wear, etc) cheap accessories selling a luxury idea, and knock-offs of young creative designers.

My favourite story regarding, I was in Paris, doing my first catwalk, ever, at **Paris Fashion week**…for a designer this is like the Oscars or Grammies. I partnered with **Chateau Fontainebleau** which was the King's old fox hunting castle, with horseshoe-shaped staircase entrance. I had a horse out front with a model on top with fire torches lining the way, and even had my friend, who played 'Little Mermaid' in

Prophetik Paris Fashion week Catwalk at Chateau Fontainebleau

the fountain for the cocktail hour. My collection was DaVinci inspired, where I made my gowns out of metal. The catwalk, which was in the old ball room, had never been walked on before by models even though it was last used royally by fashion icon **Marie Antoinette**. Well, the following day, after being named on the French news emerging designer of the year, we went to dinner to celebrate, and we ran into Ralph Lauren's design team. They were lovely 24-30 year old women with a great since of style, so we bought them wine. After the second bottle, they disclosed to me that they knew who I was, as they had my catwalk photos on their 'inspiration' board. All I could do is smile…as my hippie dad, Jim, would say: *"inspiring another is the greatest complement."* We have to slow it down and rethink fashion and give the reigns back to the "gifted" artists.

Fast Fashion was designed to accelerate supply chain efficiency by mass-producing mostly synthetic, low-quality materials with rapidity, in places like Vietnam, India and China. But its long-lasting impact was to condition consumers to wear garments only a few times, and once they're no longer 'in style', discarding the garments, to buy new items, on the cheap. In so doing, this habituation created… and continues to generate…vast landfills of synthetics-infused waste. One surprising element we discovered in the making of the documentary, when interviewing designer/co-founder of Velvet clothing, Toni Spencer, she educated us on the fact that commercial fashion companies incinerate their unused clothing for tax benefits, and to avoid mark downs. BBC covered a story finding Burberry destroyed over 90 million pounds worth of inventory over the last 5 years, showcasing

H&M accused of burning 12 tonnes of new, unsold clothing per year

FASHION | IN-DEPTH

another real issue of overproduction, with no responsibility of the waste and toxins created.

These relatively inexpensive garments might satisfy consumer addiction in the short term, but not only do they create much more textile waste, they shed fibers quickly, adding to the global micro-fiber pollution that now endangers human and environmental health.

Microscopic image of a mico-fiber from inside a fish

Plastic materials (think polyester) fragment into smaller particles, and once released into the environment, they become micro-plastics (less than 5 mm) and eventually dissolve into even smaller fragments (nano-plastics). These micro-plastics, mostly in the form of fibers, come from washing clothes, from the abrasions of garments through wear, and as a result of exposure to ultraviolet light.

Many of the chemical additives in textiles and the microfibres have been documented to have either carcinogenic (cancer causing) or endocrine disruptive (hormone confusion) effects in human and animal bodies (see Chapter 5). Once inhaled or ingested, these additives can **leach from the micro-plastic particles and expose body tissues to phthalates and bisphenol A, both notorious hormone disrupters, even at low concentrations.**[7]

 ## Another 'Skin Deep' Challenge

Beginning in the late 1990's, in concert with the 'fast fashion' trend, many clothing manufacturers started adding silver nanoparticles to all kinds of garments. These are ultra-fine particles, between 1 and 100 nanometres in size (the same dimensions as some biological molecules in the body). Research indicates they cross through the skin into cell membranes and then into body organs, to be further spread throughout the body through blood circulation.

Nano-silver particles are sometimes added to clothing as a finishing, or during the melting of plastic to create polyester, to give the garments antimicrobial, anti-odour, stain resistant and 'self-cleaning' functionality. Untold hundreds of garments embedded with nano-silver are now sold worldwide, a few common examples being socks, sports

[7] "Micro-plastics as contaminants in the marine environment: a review." Cole M. Et al. *Marine Pollution Bulletin.* 2012. Also, "From cohorts to molecules: Adverse impacts of endocrine disrupting mixtures." Caporale N. Et al. *Science.* 2022.

apparel for both men and women, trousers and shorts. These items have been manufactured and sold by such companies as Under Armour, Outlier, and Sharper Image.

Though nano-silver particles are non-chemical additives to the fibers of clothing, they mimic many of the characteristics seen with synthetic chemicals and pose many similar potential health dangers (again, see Chapter 5). Because some of the nano particles are smaller than many viruses—and because nano-particles get released during clothes washing and end up in the environment, and nano-silver can be absorbed by the skin during wear or as a result of sweating (see Chapter 4 on skin permeability) it should be needless to say that caution needs to be exercised with wearing any nano-clothing.[8]

Among the health dangers of nano-silver absorption that have surfaced in science studies is reproductive and developmental toxicity, documented in laboratory animals when they were exposed to nano-silver. The result of nano-silver exposure was testicular/sperm toxicity in males and ovarian embryonic toxicity in females, and impaired cognitive behaviour in their offspring. These results now need to be replicated in human subjects, if experiments can be designed in which harm isn't inflicted.[9]

[8] "Determination of silver nanoparticle release from antibacterial fabrics into artificial sweat." Kulthong K. Et al. *Particle and Fibre Toxicology*. 2010 April.

[9] "A review of reproductive and developmental toxicity of silver nanoparticles in laboratory animals." Ema M. Et al. *Reproductive Toxicology*. 2017 January.

Synthetic 'Natural' Becomes the New Natural

It's easy for us to focus on textile manufacturing processes that emphasise problematic synthetics while ignoring how those same manufacturers are creating their own "natural" fabric using cellulose based polymers to create the fabric and market it as sustainable. A lot of times, they name the fabric some fancy, catchy name, one they that obviously own, they leave consumers wondering: *"What is that?"* And guess who gets to define it? Yes indeed, it's the company that invested a lot of money into the development, and they even get to test it and send in their own results to the regulators.

I call these the "hybrid" fabrics…they sound good, but are they really the answer? Are they toxic free and healthy for the wearer, or they just serving up a positive in the form of less polyester? I asked this a few times to Lyocell, who owns Tencel, and never received a straight answer. I have had hundreds of my friends say they bought this bamboo sock, or this Tencel t-shirt, or PET board shorts, all professed to be a "safe" eco buying choice. Then, I must deliver the truth, and explain to them the chemical processes used to make these lab-born fabrics.

My friends thought they were doing something healthy for themselves, but they were being duped into an entry level "hybrid" clothing item. They want to buy the Tesla fabric, but without the Tesla price, and sometimes the right choice is more expensive, because of how it's made and from what it's made of. There are no shortcuts.

We are addicted to cheap price points due to the fast fashion model. I cannot make a t-shirt for the price H&M is selling their t-shirt… at $7…my fabric cost is more. Everything in life has increased in price… fuel, housing, food, even fast food, yet we're still paying the same price for a t-shirt or sweater as in the 1970s…meaning that something is off and someone is paying somehow somewhere for this cheap price. It's a cost split among poor workers, who are making the garment, the polluted country, that's allowing the manufacturer to make big bucks, and people wearing the garments, for the cheap toxic ingredients, substances outlawed in many countries, that keep the final product price down.

I once had a meeting with Levis, in San Fransisco, in which I suggested using my natural indigo dye from Tennessee instead of their synthetic dye. It would cost them $10 more per pair of jeans for my dye (at the time) or cost them 10 cents per jean to do a recycling water program for their synthetic dyes where they were manufacturing. I think most consumers would pay that extra $10.00 to know that the denim they are wearing is not dyed with something harmful. I look at synthetic dying like painting a beautiful gradient red wood wall with toxic paint…yes it is one solid colour, but the wood can no longer breathe and it off gasses. Let's also dispel a myth when the denim company says 'dyed with Indigo' it does not mean the plant, but the colour…A lovely misleading play on words. There is a reason synthetic indigo dye is only made in one country, which is China…because of the outlawed toxic ingredients which you will find out more in the documentary.

But most of these companies are run by a CEO responsible to a board (the benefactors), and generally focused on numbers. They only want to increase the bottom line, and not decrease their toxic impact, unless or until it undermines their sales. Affecting sales is what we can do to companies with toxic products if we can convince enough people through this book and the documentary that what they place on their body is just as important as what they place in their body, thus impacting change.

Can polyester underwear affect fertility, cause impotence?

"There is no doubt that it is one of the most popular synthetic materials available almost everywhere, but based on studies, polyester should not touch your skin," said Dr Akta Bajaj, senior consultant and head-obstetrics, gynaecology, Ujala Cygnus Group of Hospitals

LOCAL NEWS ›

Your athletic wear could contain high levels of BPA: Here's a list of brands affected

KCAL NEWS

By KCAL-News Staff
May 18, 2023 / 10:07 AM PDT / CBS/CNN

A growing number of sports bras, shirts and leggings brands found with high levels of toxic chemical, watchdog warns

By Parija Kavilanz, CNN
6 minute read · Updated 4:15 PM EDT, Thu May 18, 2023

What Science Journals Say About 'Natural' Fibers

"Natural fibers have been coated with chemicals for e.g. colouring, waterproofing, or durability, {they then} lose their naturalness and become synthetic fibers…detached from textile garments primarily through washing," declared a study in 2016, *in Environmental Science & Technology.*[10]

Or this one: *"Natural and semisynthetic microfibres have often been excluded from studies with the assumption that non-plastic fibers are readily biodegradable and/or harmless in the environment. Although nature and semisynthetic fibers can break down more quickly than synthetic polymers, these fibers can persist from months to decades in aquatic systems depending on the microfibre types and environmental factors. Dyes and treatments may also prolong fiber persistence in the environment,"* noted a 2021 article in *Environmental Technology & Chemistry.*[11]

It's become increasingly clear over the past two decades that despite being derived from natural materials, 'natural' fibers often contain a mind-numbing array of chemical additives, dyes, and finishing agents added during production. These can include toxic compounds like bisphenol, azo dyes, polyfluorinated alkyl compounds (PFAS), and formaldehyde. Other additives to 'natural fibers' range from flame retardants and antimicrobial chemicals to ultraviolet light

---

[10] "Microfibre Masses Recovered from Conventional Machine Washing of New or Aged Garments." Hartline N.L. Et al. *Environmental Science & Technology*, 2016.

[11] "Are We Underestimating Antropogenic Microfiber Pollution? A Critical Review of Occurrence, Methods, and Reporting." Athey SN. Erdle LM. *Environmental Toxicology & Chemistry*. 2021 July.

stabilisers. All of these are added so consumers can be marketed with the manufacturer's message that "our garments will give you any desired properties you can imagine."

During garment manufacturing countless fibers are released and become airborne. Many more fibers get released during the washing and drying of each garment, and more with normal abrasion release from daily wear.

Released with the fibers are the synthetic chemicals, composing the colorants and pigments that had been applied to garments by either being mixed with melted polymers, or by being added to fibers, using a variety of techniques, the most popular being batch-dyeing, in which fibers, fabrics, or garments are submerged in a dye solution.

"The residues of these compounds (which tend not to be biodegradable) may be discharged directly into the environment where they spread, even entering the food chain. Many of these chemicals are hazardous to human health," according to a 2015 science study.[12]

[12] "Human health risk associated with brominated flame-retardants." Lyche JL. Et al. *Environ Int.* 2015.

Wastewater, containing these dyes, is generally treated before disposal in most European countries, though many other textile-producing countries throughout the world allow wastewater to be dumped directly into streams, lakes and oceans, causing ecosystem degradation and harm to aquatic life.[13]

Long after disposal in landfills, textiles continue to release both synthetic and 'natural' fibers (and the toxins contained within) into the air and groundwater. Just as there are 'forever' chemicals that remain toxic for a lifetime, the poisons that keep on giving, so, too, can entire garments become 'forever' for generations to come.

As you will see in, subsequent chapters of this handbook, clothing manufacturing processes that deceive consumers extends beyond fast fashion, nano-particles, synthetic 'natural' fibers, into a hide-and-seek game of synthetic chemical toxins hidden in garments, and a deficit of truth-telling about which toxins are most dangerous for human and environmental health.

NEWS

Nov. 11, 2008 -- The secret is out for one of the world's most recognizable lingerie brands, according to a potential class action lawsuit in which consumers claim they've experienced very uncomfortable symptoms, like rashes, hives and permanent scarring from **Victoria's Secret bras**.

"I had the welts ... very red, hot to the touch, extremely inflamed, blistery. It itched profusely," said Roberta Ritter, who describes herself as a longtime Victoria's Secret shopper. "I couldn't sleep, waking up itching.

"I was just utterly sick," she added.

---

[13] "LCA benchmarking study on textiles made of cotton, polyester, nylon, acryl, or elastane." Van der Velden NM. Et al. *Int J Life Cycle Assess*. 2014.

We Don't Know the Real Harm Being Done

"Synthetic-chemical production levels overall have been doubling every decade since the 1940s. At least five new synthetic chemicals are developed for commercial use every single day, yet no one has any realistic idea how harmful these chemicals are to us, either alone or acting in synergy with other chemicals. Our ignorance on these matters long ago surpassed our wisdom." *–The Hundred-Year Lie: How to Protect Yourself from the Chemicals that are Destroying Your Health. Randall Fitzgerald,*

Cara Delevingne at her first catwalk show walking for Jeff at London fashion week

 Chapter III: Playing Hide and Seek with Toxins

 Harms Finally Coming Out of Closets

"Little has been done to disclose the potentially harmful compounds hiding in our closet...non-targeted analysis {using an ultrasonic extraction} of a set of 60 garments {most polyester apparel produced in China} revealed the presence of thousands of compounds, among which over a hundred chemicals were tentatively identified...These included substances known to have risks for reproduction toxicity, carcinogens and irritants."[1]

---

[1] "Chemicals in textiles: A potential source for human exposure and environmental pollution." Giovanna Luongo. Department of Environmental Science and Analytical Chemistry. Stockholm University. 2015

Rigging the Hide & Seek Game

€very meeting I go to, by midway the person typically says something to the effect of: *"I had no idea what to wear today to meet you…I was so worried, not knowing what my clothes were made of."* After meeting my mate, Darin Olien, co-host of *'Down to Earth with Zac Efron'*, for his health podcast, he immediately asked me to make him some clothes for the second season, which I designed. Now Darin speaks about it in his book *'Fatal Conveniences'* and has been converted forever and decided to join us in the documentary discovery.

When was the last time you took an inventory of your entire wardrobe? By that I mean, when did you inspect each article of clothing to identify the fabric fibers used to produce it? Is it 100% silk or cotton, or mixed with a synthetic, non-breathable fabric, like nylon or acrylic?

If you're like most people, your answer would be that you've rarely paid much attention. Maybe you just automatically trust the clothing brand. Constant exposure causes acceptance, and as consumers, we have an automatic trust in that if something is being sold to us from a store, someone has checked that garment to make sure it is safe for us to wear. However, that is not the case. Also, something most people don't know, as a designer I make my own content labels, meaning I can list whatever I want it to say and no one checks the accuracy. Imagine that 100% cashmere sweater. Is it truly 100% or might it have an acrylic mix? Only a designer's eye, an expert's touch, or a burn test could really discern the truth. Some fabrics are "worth" more in price than others and I have seen the rayons labeled as silk, etc. Now we know why those recycling programs are not working in the textile world, for no one knows the true makeup. Did you know acrylic was designed in the 50s for stay-at home moms to not have to hand wash those beautiful wool sweaters? I don't think any mom would trade wool for acrylic, if she knew what those chemicals do to their kids.

Because the identities of most synthetic chemical toxins added during manufacturing don't appear on garment labels, trying to establish which articles of clothing hide which specific chemicals might seem to require something approaching paranormal powers.

Step one in any self-education process about toxic clothing involves realizing and accepting this truism: *the more synthetic clothing you possess and regularly wear, the more synthetic chemicals you're absorbing through your skin, and the more health repercussions you can expect over a lifetime. It is called bioaccumulation and the idea is to lesson your exposure as much as possible.*

One solution is to lab test your clothing to identify toxins, but that requires sophisticated technology and thousands of dollars to finance each test, obviously an unaffordable option for most people. It costs us about $1,800 for each fabric we tested for only 5-10 different toxins and there are thousands used in clothing manufacturing. Plus you must know what to test for. Given that vacuum we must rely on lab testing conducted by university scientists, environmental and consumer health organizations, and government agencies, to identify and alert us to potential toxic dangers in our clothing and other products. Since the industry is self-regulating you can imagine how much is not tested and the testing facilities are very pro-company meaning they passed several things we tested that had known carcinogens…So, who is really protecting us?

Let's start with what we already do know from research released thus far. This information should give you some glimpses at what you should be watching for in your clothing choices.

Swiss Government Agency Lab Results

Five scientists with a Swiss government regulatory agency examined 150 textile samples taken randomly from Swiss retail outlets and online shops and tested the fabrics for a variety of toxins, including *azo dyes*, the most widely used chemical class of textile dyes, which are banned in clothing in the European Union.

One-quarter of the analyzed clothing samples contained toxins suspected of being mutagenic, meaning capable of inducing genetic mutations in DNA. Garments analyzed in this study were *socks, underwear, T-shirts, children's clothing and sports clothing*. These were common-brand garments (65 brands), carrying affordable prices, made from cotton or polyester and polyamide, and sold in mainstream retail outlets. Most were manufactured in China or Bangladesh.

Studies *"have shown the ability of skin bacteria to reductively cleave to the azo bonds of azo dyes, releasing AAs (aromatic amines) which may then be absorbed through skin. In the European Union, 22 of these AAs are classified as carcinogens and banned for use in azo dyes in textiles"* with direct and prolonged skin contact.

Among clothing samples tested, many of the positive ones had two or more different amines. *Polyester T-shirts* for kids have seven amines including the most toxic ones, aniline and p-phenylenediamine. *Bras* made of polyester and polyamide blends were also egregious offenders. Dark clothing items that are made of polyester were the biggest toxic offenders. One known mutagen was found in 16 samples of garments made of cotton and other cellulose based fibers.

*"**O**ur results show that a substantial number of coloured textiles contained non-regulated AAs of toxicological concerns…there is an obvious **need to assess consumer health risks for these non-regulated AAs and to fill the gap in the regulation of clothing textiles**…this survey clearly shows that a substantial percentage of azo dyes used in today's clothing textiles consists of hazardous AAs."[2]*

 ## Swedish University Lab Findings on Clothing Toxins

Four scientists from Stockholm University selected twenty-six clothing samples of various textile materials and colours manufactured in 14 different countries {and} analyzed the clothing using liquid chromatography tandem mass spectrometry. Among the investigated textile products, 11 clothes were for babies, toddlers, and children. Eight of the 11 compounds included in the investigation were detected

---

[2] "Survey on hazardous non-regulated aromatic amines as cleavage products of azo dyes found in clothing textiles on the Swiss Market." Crettaz S. Et al. *Journal of Consumer Protection and Food Safety*. 2019 August.

in the textiles. Benzothiazole was present in 23 of 26 investigated garments.

The samples covered 14 of the most common clothing brands sold in Sweden and included T-shirts and Jeans manufactured in 14 different countries. The two chemicals searched for—benzothiazoles (BTs) and benzotriazoles (BTris)—are widely used to prevent yellowing degradation in clothing. Both are suspected carcinogens, and residues of these chemicals are often found in wastewater, a result of clothes laundering.

The highest concentration of BT turned up in *white soccer shorts* made from 100% polyester. The second highest concentration appeared in *blue blouses* made from 100% polyester. Ironically, the third highest concentration was measured in a *red baby garment* "made from 'organic cotton' and marked with 'Nordic Ecolabel,'" supposedly indicating the clothing item was safe for human and environmental health.

"The knowledge of the actual content of harmful chemicals in clothes distributed and retailed on the common market is highly insufficient. This is due to difficulties to obtain information on what substances that actually have been used and especially the lack of analytical date of chemicals present in clothing textiles. Investigating the levels of different chemicals present in clothes is of great importance, as clothing textiles can be a possible route for human exposure to these {toxic} compounds by skin contact."[3]

 ## Three Research Centres Document Clothing Toxins

Eight scientists from research centres in Australia, Italy and The Netherlands investigated the presence of PFAS (per- and polyfluoroalkyl chemicals) in 15 categories of consumer products, ranging from cosmetics and hygiene products to electronics, using High-Resolution Mass Spectrometry, and found the highest diversity of PFAS in textiles, where the chemicals are used to produce water-resistant and stain-resistant clothing.[4]

As a starter, it's become well-known that PFAS are a class of synthetics known as 'forever chemicals' because they can accumulate over time in human and animal body tissues and they can persist in the environment for hundreds of years. Science studies have indicated that PFAS exposure in humans can lead to DNA damage, liver damage, thyroid disease, obesity, fertility issues and cancer. So, it's noteworthy that the authors of this 2023 study specifically mentioned how clothing "worn directly and for extended periods, such as *school uniforms*, have a high potential to be a significant source of exposure."

---

[3] "Benzothiazole, benzotriazole, and their derivatives in clothing textile—a potential source of environmental pollutants and human exposure." Avagyan R. Et al. Environ Sci Pollut Res Int. 2015 April.

[4] Writing in a 2023 issue of the *Journal of Hazardous Materials Letters*, this science team made a series of disturbing revelations.

Quite remarkably, according to this report, the earliest study on PFAS-containing products wasn't conducted anywhere in the world until 2009, when the U.S. Environmental Protection Agency did an analysis of PFAS appearing in products. Considering how dangerous these chemicals can be, and how widely they appear in consumer products, particularly in mainstream clothing, that oversight seems to be another instance of gross negligence on the part of the science and health communities and the clothing industry.[5]

 ## Environmental Group Identifies Toxic Clothes

Twenty global fashion brands—including *Levi's, Armani and Zara*-- were investigated for the presence of toxic chemicals in their clothing. Investigators purchased 141 clothing items throughout the world in 2012, that had been manufactured in 18 different countries. However, *"the place of manufacture was not identified for 25 {clothing items} which is symptomatic of an industry that is not as transparent about its manufacturing practices as it should be."*

Clothing items such as J*eans, trousers, t-shirts, dresses and underwear*, made from both synthetic and natural fabrics, for men, women and children, were tested for the presence of phthalates and nonylphenol ethoxylates (NPEs). (Note: Studies have linked phthalates to breast cancer, type 2 diabetes, obesity, asthma and endocrine disorders; other research has found NPEs toxic to aquatic life.)

---

[5] "Per- and polyfluoroalkyl substances (PFAS) in consumer products: Current knowledge and research gaps." Dewapriya P. Et al. *Journal of Hazardous Materials Letters*. 2023 November.

Alarming findings of this Greenpeace science investigation:

() **NPEs turned up in 63% of all the clothing items tested,** ranging from 1 part per million to 45,000 parts per million.

() **All of the 20 clothing brands had one or more items containing NPEs**; one or more NPEs appeared in items from 13 of the 18 garment manufacturing countries.

() **Highest concentrations of NPEs—above 1,000 parts per million—** were found in the brands *C&A, Mango, Levi's, Calvin Klein, Zara, Metersbonwe, Jack & Jones, and Marks & Spencer.*

() **All 31 items with plastisol printed fabric contained phthalates**; very high concentrations of phthalates turned up in two garments manufactured for *Tommy Hilfiger, one for Armani, and one for Victoria's Secret.*

    Part of the blame for the presence of these chemicals in the tested clothing was placed by Greenpeace on the global 'fast fashion' trend in which suppliers are pressured to meet ever-tighter deadlines to manufacture and supply clothing, *"which encourages irresponsible practices and the cutting of corners in terms of environmental and labor costs."* Additional blame went to **'greenwashers'**—brands that have expressed zero toxin intentions, yet have not lived up to their anti-toxin public pledges. Singled out were Levi's and G-Star Raw brands.[6]

6 "Toxic Threads: The Big Fashion Stitch-Up." Greenpeace International. 2012.

Gap, Old Navy Apparel Flagged in Toxic-Chemical Investigation

BY JASMIN MALIK CHUA ⊡   MAY 6, 2022 6:07PM

 ## Toxins That Are Found *Everywhere*

Everywhere you look certain toxins have become so ubiquitous that you'll detect them, if you have access to the right testing equipment. A good example is the antibacterial and anti-fungicidal finish chemical called triclosan.

It's a proven hormone disrupter and it produces chloroform. This is the synergy part I have been speaking about. When the UV rays hit this chemical, it converts to Dioxin. **Dioxin** is the chemical present in the notorious **Agent Orange,** which has been linked to **breast cancer, liver damage, and nervous disorders**. The press calls it **"the most toxic man-made chemical"**.

The Danish EPA measured Triclosan levels in clothes up to 195 parts per million (ppm). Triclosan has been shown to rapidly react with chlorinated water to produce chloroform (trichloromethane). **Dioxin is also found in synthetic dyes.**

Fibers and polymers that have been impregnated with triclosan have names such as Ultra-Fresh, Amicor, Microban, Monolith, Bactonix and Sanitized. In a study of streams across the USA, triclosan was found in 57.6% of the 139 streams tested at a median concentration of 140 ng/L. Triclosan accumulates in fatty tissue and has been found in human breast milk and urine samples.

This chemical is so problematic for human health that in September 2016, the **U.S. Food and Drug Administration banned triclosan** from soap products following a risk assessment that it **penetrates the skin and can cause hormone disruption** that could potentially trigger breast cancer and other health problems.[7]

Yes, you read that correctly! **Triclosan has been outlawed in soap products that bring the chemical in direct contact with human skin,** *but not in clothing that brings the chemical in contact with human skin.* How insane is that? There is no rhyme or reason to such irregular regulations.

Among clothing items where you might find and absorb triclosan: Aprons, Athletic wear & athletic shirts, Bibs, Caps, Coat shells & fill, Dresses, Gloves, Golf shirts, Gowns, Hosiery, Incontinence care products, Intimate apparel, Running gear, Shoes & insoles, Sleepwear, Socks, Sports apparel, Sweatshirts, Underwear, Uniforms, Wet suits.[8]

---

[7] "Triclosan Exposure, Transformation, and Human Health Effects." Weatherly LM. Gosse JA. J Toxicol Environ Health B Crit Rev. 2017.

[8] --Environmental Working Group, https://www.ewg.org/consumer-guides/where-triclosan-still-approved-use.

 ## Toxins in Clothes---A Deeper Dive

Note to Readers: Below is a representative sampling of science study testing results on specific items of clothing. (Meaning there are too many to list!)

 Baby & Child Clothing

In 2022, the U.S. consumer health organization, Environmental Working Group, commissioned an independent laboratory to test for PFAS, (which stands for **P**oly**F**luoro**A**lkyl **S**ubstances) the so-called 'forever chemicals', in baby and children's textiles. PFAS were added to make the garments resistant to water, stain, and grease. **All 34 fabric samples contained fluorine**, which indicates the presence of PFAS, and 10 of the fabrics had detectable levels of individuals PFAS.

The types of products and brands tested included *swimwear by Carter's and Disney, and a hat by Carter's, and raincoats by Carter's, The North Face, Columbia and Hatley.* The items had been purchased online from Amazon, Target and Old Navy. These were especially disturbing findings for children, no matter what the levels of PFAS,

Backstage Prophetik catwalk LFW 'Nevermore' Intimates

because "the bodies of babies and young children are still developing, {making them} among the most vulnerable to harms from PFAS."[9]

It's funny how kids can influence parents to do strange things for them. I designed a kids collection called 'Sustainable Kids' for my daughter Bella back in the early 2000s, and sold the line in Nordstroms. I could not find anything to purchase that was not up to par for my Bella, so I created hemp skinny pants for the boys and reversible cotton/ hemp dresses for the girls. I even made Bella her first hemp training

---

[9] "New baby textile product tests show concerning levels of toxic 'forever chemicals'." Environmental Working Group. November 3, 2022.

bra. I believe that if you can teach them young how something should feel on your body and how it should be made, it will positively impact them for the future. I miscalculated that it's not cool for designer dad to make his daughter's first training bra out of hemp! I even mentioned we could do a bra hemp dye party with her girlfriends…yep that did not fly either!

 Bras

Six Chinese scientists writing in the science journal, *Chemosphere*, revealed in late 2023 how they had tested a range of brassiere samples manufactured and sold in five areas of China, to determine their content of heavy metals left over as residues from the manufacturing process.

"Carcinogenic risks from the metals in 5% of brassiere samples exceed the acceptable level," the scientists reported about the 86 bras tested. That meant **five bras could potentially trigger cancer.** The heavy metals tested at the highest levels in the bras were antimony and nickel.

It was speculated in the study that a high absorption of the metals occurred among users of the bras due to the variety of bra colours, indicating differences in dyeing and other production processes resulting in metals being added to the bras.

"This come from the occurrence, and potential release, of heavy metals in female underwear manufactured in China: Implication for

women's health."[10] Antimony is a metalloid, like arsenic, used as a catalyst in the production of polyester. It has been linked to cancer risks in humans, **potentially including breast cancer as a result of absorption of the heavy metal from bras into breast tissue.**[11]

Nickel is used in textile dye processes. **Exposure to nickel, because it's a metalloestrogen** (a binder to oestrogen receptors in breast tissue), **and has been linked to breast cancer** in some science studies.[12]

Prophetik Bras made of Scottish cotton lace & org cotton/hemp
models: Maria Amanda & Caroline Schaub

 ## Children's School Apparel/Uniforms

As a single dad bringing up my daughter in the fashion industry, I obviously had an issue the day I placed her into a private school, where they mandated polyester, synthetically dyed fashion made in

---

[10] Chen H. Et al. Chemosphere. 2023 November.

[11] "Interactions of antimony with biomolecules and its effects on human health." Lai Z. Et al. *Ecotoxicology and Environmental Safety*. 2022 March.

[12] "The role of cadmium and nickel in oestrogen receptor signalling and breast cancer: metalloestrogen or not?" Aquino NB. Et al. J Environ Sci Health C Environ Carcinog Ecotoxicol Rev. 2012.

China and consisted of a polyester, printed plaid- pleated skirt (printed with plastisol ink which contain PFAS) and a polyester dyed polo shirt. It is my job to protect my child yet due to this mandate she could not attend unless she wore the chemically- induced uniform that would affect her growth, her hormones, her skin, and her overall health wearing it eight hours a day plus physical education sweating in it.

I fought the school and they refused my ply… strangely I was doing a catwalk for Prince Albert for the Princess Grace Foundation in Monaco that year at Hotel de Paris. I was invited after my catwalk from an owner of one of the big yachts in the harbour…he obviously wanted me to bring my fashion models with me. So, a small group of us went to experience this Monaco life. The older gentleman knew I was from Tennessee and said his kids live in TN. We quickly discovered that his grandkids and my daughter attended the same private christian school.

'Princess Grace Collection' at Hotel De Paris, Monaco, Sept. 14, 2012

I asked him what he did for a living and he said he owned the educational school uniform company that actually supplied the uniforms for the school! I then asked him did he have any remorse for poisoning his grandkids? He laughed and said, *"look around you."* I knew at this point I was fighting an uphill battle if one would even knowingly poison his own grandkids for profit. In the aftermath of that disturbing encounter, I made a kid's collection, called 'Sustainable Kids' sold in Nordstrom featuring a hemp t-shirt printed with our organic pigment ink with the quote: 'Don't poison the grandchildren."

The school uniform companies have an agreement with the schools, which gives them 'kickbacks' on the purchase of the mandated official uniforms. I even offered to design & produce the uniforms for free out of hemp and natural dyes but was kindly rejected.

It was a battle this single dad could not win at the time, and to think I was the crazy one, so I just had my daughter wear a natural garment underneath her uniform, avoiding the uniform to rub her skin.

A 12-person team of scientists acquired 72 items of children's clothing, including school uniforms, from stores in Canada and the U.S. and subjected the garments to lab testing for the presence of PFAS, the 'forever chemicals' used in manufacturing to impart stain resistance. **PFAS were detected in all 72 products** from both countries.

"Total targeted PFAS levels in school uniforms were significantly higher than in other {clothing} items," reported the scientists in a 2022 issue of Environmental Science Technology.

"Clothing may be an important source of direct human exposure {to PFAS toxins}, especially for children."[13]

Another testing survey from 2022 searched for the presence of eight heavy metals in new preschool-children's clothing manufactured in four Asian regions (China, South Korea, India and Indonesia.) Clothes tested included short-sleeve shirts, shorts, long-sleeve shirts, trousers, underwear and socks.

Long-sleeve shirts for boys and girls contained the highest carcinogenic risks. **Both arsenic and cadmium tested at "less than acceptable levels" within the garments.** [14]

 Firefighter Clothes

Diane Cotter watched helplessly as her husband, Paul, a lieutenant with the Massachusetts Worcester Fire Department, began to deteriorate after his prostate cancer diagnosis. On a hunch that chemicals might have triggered his cancer, Diane inspected his protective pants and found quarter and dime size-sized holes in the

---

[13] "Per- and Polyfluoroalkyl Substances in North American School Uniforms." Xia C. Et al. *Environmental Science Technology*. 2022.

[14] "Occurrence and health implications of heavy metals in preschool children's clothing manufactured in four Asian regions." Chen H. Et al. *Ectoxiciology and Environmental Safety*. 2022 October.

crotch area. *"Holy cow,"* she told herself, *"this is how all these chemicals got into his body."*

What Diane had uncovered was an entranceway for PFAS synthetic chemicals leaching from the pants into her husband's body. These toxic chemicals were added to the uniform to protect firefighters from heat, liquids and smoke, but **since PFAS had been added to fire-fighting textiles, cancer had become responsible for killing two out of every three firefighters after the year 2002**, according to statistics which were compiled by the *"International Association of Fire Fighters."* (Firefighters in Europe had been abandoning the use of PFAS clothing after research emerged about its dangers.)

When Diane failed to get clear answers about the presence of PFAS from her inquiries to clothing manufacturers, she contacted Dr. Graham Peaslee at the University of Notre Dame. He tested the gear and published a study in 2020 about his findings in the science journal, *Environmental Science & Technology Letters*. He found "high levels" of PFAS in the textiles and because *"of the documented adverse health effects of PFAS,"* he concluded a **link to cancer** may exist.[15]

Childhood leukemia linked to PFAS exposure

December 20, 2023

Photo by National Cancer Institute on Unsplash

[15] "Another Pathway for Firefighter Exposure to Per- and Polyfluoroalkyl Substances: Firefighter Textiles." Peaslee GF. Et al. Environ Sci Technol Letter. 2020.

Monica DeCrescentis (Delta flight attendant) who blew the whistle on the uniforms

Flight Crew Uniforms

Lab-testing of airline flight-crew uniforms by four scientists at the Harvard School of Public Health, documented how health problems reported by flight attendants at Alaska Airlines could be traced to synthetic chemicals in their new uniforms. After the introduction of new uniforms an epidemic of health complaints poured in about multiple chemical sensitivity, rashes and hives, blurred vision, ear pain, sinus congestion, shortness of breath, and other conditions.

One clue about a possible cause of health complaints came from identifying the new uniform fabrics: skirts were 48% polyester, blazers 53% polyester, shirts 40% Polyester, Sweaters 55% acrylic and 22% nylon, and pants 53% polyester with a 100% polyester lining. Three of the uniform garments were assembled in China. The other two came from Indonesia. The study's authors attributed the health symptoms to chemicals added to the polyesters, such as formaldehyde, (used to make the clothes wrinkle resistant), and synthetic dyes.[16]

(Similar health problems were reported by flight attendants at American Airlines after new uniforms were introduced at that airline.)

At Delta Airlines the Flight Attendant's Union began to hear complaints from members in 2018, when new uniforms using Lands End fabrics caused allergic reactions, ranging from severe rashes to hair loss. Though Delta corporate executives claimed the uniforms were safe and not the cause of health complaints, the 'Flight Attendant's Union' paid to send uniforms samples to five testing labs.

In 2020, the Union shared the flight uniform toxicology results with its membership. Here is a listing of the clothing items tested they tested and the lab findings.

Flight Apron: **Toxic fluorinated chemicals called PFOA were found in the fabric along with stain retardants**. There is evidence that the chemicals can be carcinogenic to humans. The Union recommendation was to *"stop wearing the apron and dispose of it."*

Women's Red Outerwear Coat: **PFOA and other stain retardants were found, as well as hexavalent chromium.** These are carcinogens. The Union recommendation was to "stop wearing the red coat and dispose of it."

---

16 "Uniforms may be making flight attendants sick." Harvard T.H. Chan School of Public Health. 2019. And, "Symptoms related to new flight attendant uniforms." McNeeley E. Et al. BMC Public Health. 2018.

IFS Executive Dress: **Hexavalent chromium, a carcinogen and allergen, was detected.** The Union recommendation was to "stop wearing the executive dress and dispose of it."

Women's Wool-Blend Suiting Pants: **Total chromium at levels above maximum for fabrics was found.** The Union recommendation was: *"if you think you are reacting to the wool-blend pants, stop wearing them."*

Women's and Men's Thistle-Pink Shirts: Both the men's and women's shirts **contained formaldehyde**, though it was within allowable limits, even though formaldehyde is a carcinogenic. The Union recommendation was: *"if you experience irritant or allergic symptoms when wearing the shirts, switching to 'untreated' shirts would be a good option."*

World / United States & Canada

Flight attendants sue Delta Air Lines over 'toxic' new uniforms

- The uniforms were created by fashion designer Zac Posen and unveiled in May 2018
- Delta employees said they suffered from a range of issues, including severe respiratory illnesses, rashes, blisters, boils and hair loss

Obviously, I like to 'get my hands dirty,' so I also tested a bit of the flight uniform from the original Zac Posen design at an independent lab for the documentary. We found **898 ppm (parts per million) of toxic Fluorinated chemicals,** a strong PFAS indicator, when the "legal" limit in California, starting in January 2025 is 100 PPM[17]. As a

---

[17] See California Health & Safety Code § 108970(g).

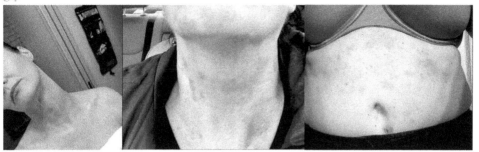

Images from Monica of Delta airline employees with rashes from the uniform

designer, with a similar background as Zac, I knew within the first year what my fabrics and dyes were made of. And, being a Tennessee farm boy, I did not like the dark toxicity of the industry, yet, I wanted to create and design beauty! I would not design, if I had to use synthetic fabrications and dyes, because my moral compass would not allow me to knowingly create something that could hurt someone wearing it.

This is not an education issue, it's an ethical issue. With this philosophy, it has taught me to seek out other ways, fabrics, dyes, and alternatives, which do exist, but obviously aren't easy to use or lucrative right now. I hope this book will inspire other designers to follow this lead and not settle for profit over people.

For the documentary, we interviewed a Delta flight attendant, Monica DeCrescentis, who originally filed the lawsuit against Lands End, which produced for, Zac Posen, the Delta Airlines uniform that caused skin rashes, headaches, fatigue and other issues. Monica shared evidence with photos, how the dye in the uniform transferred onto her body, sheets, towels, cell phone cover and shower. Her interview was very moving as neither Lands End nor Zac Posen wanted to take any responsibility for their health problems. Delta quickly moved to an OKEA textile-certified uniform for Delta employees. My personal opinion is that Delta Airlines was not aware of what was in their uniform. As a designer & manufacturer it is our responsibility to our client to inform them of what's in the makeup of what we are designing. To pretend like one does not know what is in the synthetic dyes and polyester of this uniform is like the tobacco companies saying they do not know what makes up the cigarette. Ignorance is bliss!

 ## ⚜ (Military Uniforms

Military commanders in Iraq during 2006 '**banned Marine Corps personnel from wearing synthetic athletic clothing containing polyester and nylon because of burn risks associated with the garments.**' These synthetic fibers and the chemicals within them burn quickly and intensely when exposed to incendiaries, fusing fabric to skin. Under Armour t-shirts were of particular concern.[18]

The military also coats their uniforms with flame retardants that contain PFAS. Golden Manufacturing, based in Mississippi, has been

[18] "Marines in Iraq warned of risks with synthetic clothes." Patrick Dickson. *Stars and Stripes*. April 14, 2006.

producing products for the US Military since 1970, and the plant manager of Golden quoted in his local paper, *"Many items are shipped out to get coated by the fire-retardant spray."*

Militaries in other countries have admitted a range of problems with synthetic chemicals in their uniforms. In Sweden, for instance, soldiers home on leave from Afghanistan were forbidden to wear their desert uniforms around civilian or family members, because the fabrics were impregnated with permethrin, a toxic insect repellant. (U.S. military uniforms also contain permethrin, as do some outdoor clothing.) Swedish public health authorities called permethrin potentially carcinogenic and a neurotoxin, but the Swedish military claimed the toxins were in uniforms at such low levels they were safe for soldiers to wear, just not around non-military people.[19]

 Outdoor Wear

Those 'forever chemicals', called PFAS, used to make clothing both water and stain resistant (even though the chemicals can cause cancer and suppress the immune system) showed up in 15 of 20 outdoor clothing items tested by the consumer health group, the Seattle-based Toxic-Free Future, in a 2022 study. Most outdoor jackets, 9 of 13, harboured PFAS, as did three of four pairs of outdoor pants, and three out of three outdoor shirts.

---

[19] "Swedish soldiers wear 'toxic' uniforms: report." Rebecca Martin. The Local Se. Oct. 30, 2012.

Garner's hemp boxers logwood & indigo plant dye at his redwood cabin

Older PFAS that are banned in the European Union and were supposed to have been phased out by U.S. manufacturers years ago, nonetheless, turned up in the lab tests. Since all of the tested items were manufactured in Asia, and product labels didn't disclose the presence of PFAS, it's possible the anti-toxin laws and standards were being intentionally circumvented, with U.S. retailers failing to exercise proper oversight.

In a study released by Toxic-Free Future, Both newer (PFAS spinoffs) and older PFAS compounds showed up in *Under Armour women's anorak jackets, REI Co-op Westwinds GTX jackets for women, REI Rainwall jackets for children, 5.11 tactical women's stain resistant shirts, and Rothco tactical duty pants* for men and women. Older (and more dangerous) PFAS also turned up in *Dakine Women's Noella Tech*

Flannel Button Down shirts and Lelinta Men's Casual trousers, whereas only newer PFAS was found in *Patagonia Torrentshell* jackets for women. Many of these items were being sold by Walmart stores.[20]

 ## Underwear (Men)

An animal study tested the effects of wearing either *polyester or cotton* underpants over 24 months, on sperm and testicular health of males. In the polyester group **"there was a significant decrease in sperm count and motile sperms, with an increase in abnormal forms, and the testicular biopsy showed degenerative changes."** No such toxic effects were seen in the cotton underpants.[21]

A second study, this time with 50 human males, had them wear underpants made of either 100% polyester, a 50/50 polyester/cotton blend, 100% cotton, or 100% wool. Testing of sexual activity was done at 6 and 12 months of wearing the under garments. **Sexual activity was "significantly reduced" during the time period studied in men who wore the polyester** and the polyester/cotton mix underwear, compared to the cotton and wool wearers who showed insignificant changes. The polyester underwear generated electrostatic field effects on the pubic area of wearers, whereas the other fabric types did not, which could be significant.[22]

---

[20] "New study finds toxic chemicals in most products labeled stain- or water-resistant." Toxic-Free Future. 01/26/22

[21] "Effect of different types of textile fabric on spermatogenesis: an experimental study." Shafik A. *Urology Research.* 1993.

[22] "Effect of different types of textiles on male sexual activity." Shafik A. *Archives of Andrology.* 1996.

Prophetik hemp boxers dyed with eucalyptus leaves in Malibu

A Third study discovered that '**wearing a polyester sling acted as a cheap contraceptive!**' Fertile men can be rendered azoospermic by the creation of an electrostatic field across the scrotum and the disorderly thermoregulation created by the polyester! I guess that explains why I conceived my first child, Isabella, the day I lost my virginity! And, actually, my second child, Veda, as well! Go hemp boxers![23]

My favorite association came as a kid, when I would run across the horrible 80's polyester carpet in the den and shock my sister. Polyester is hydrophobic in nature and doesn't allow moisture to pass, therefore, it attracts and detracts positive and negative, creating an electrostatic discharge. The result can be infertility as it shocks your scrotum which is the thinnest layer of skin.

Prophetik's London Fashion week catwalk 'Nevermore' collection

⚜ Underwear (Women)

Samples of unworn *Thinx and Lunapads menstrual underwear* were sent for testing by "University of Notre Dame" professor, Graham Peaslee, of the 'Department of Chemistry and Biochemistry'. **Peaslee's lab found *high levels of fluorine, a strong PFAS indicator*, in a pair of women's Thinx** and in a pair of a Thinx brand that is marketed to teenage girls. Experts believe that high levels of organic fluorine, suggest that the underwear was intentionally manufactured with PFAS, the 'forever chemical.'

Lunapads, manufactured in Canada, didn't show evidence of PFAS, a known endocrine system-disrupting toxin. The Thinx underwear had been sold as 'organic cotton' but apparently still had finishes and coatings containing PFAS added to the fabrics.[24]

VOGUE

Thinx settled a lawsuit over chemicals in its period underwear. *"Through its uniform, widespread nationwide advertising campaign, [Thinx] has led consumers to believe that Thinx Underwear is a safe, healthy and sustainable choice for women, and that it is free of harmful chemicals,"* read the complaint

---

[24] "Toxic PFAS Chemicals Found in Period-Proof Underwear." The Environmental Working Group. February 20, 2020.

filed in May 2022.[25] In reality, Thinx underwear contains harmful chemicals which are a safety hazard to the female body and the environment.

A 2023 study tested for **the prevalence of eight heavy metals in female underwear manufactured in China**, finding that *"the detection frequency of each metal was more than 70%, suggesting a widespread presence of these metals in female underwear,"* according to the study authors. **Lead** was the heavy metal with the highest concentration in all 41 samples of women's underwear that was manufactured in five areas of China.

These findings alarmed the study scientists (all Chinese) because *"underwear is a potential source of women's exposure to heavy metals owing to its direct contact with the skin, especially the skin of the vagina and vulva, which has a strong absorptive capacity."* The science team also measured the migration rates of the heavy metals from the underwear into skin and found copper, arsenic, nickel and cadmium had the highest rates of absorption into female organs.

Chronic **exposure through underwear** to these toxic metals can cause a range of health hazards, even at low levels of exposure, including **neurocognitive impairment, metabolic disorders, cardiovascular and renal diseases, and many types of cancers.**[26]

---

[25] https://www.courtlistener.com/docket/63337079/1/dickens-v-thinx-inc/

[26] "Occurrence and potential release of heavy metals in female underwear manufactured in China: Implication for women's health." Chen H. Et al. Chemosphere. 2023 November.

Socks

In a series of laboratory tests, done during 2021, the "Center for Environmental Health", a consumer group based in California, discovered more than 100 brands of socks to be testing over the safe limits of exposure to bisphenol A (BPA), an endocrine system-disrupting chemical which is added to synthetic fabrics to improve their strength and lifespan. The BPA toxin was found mainly in socks made of polyester, with spandex. None was found in cotton socks. The toxin is known to leach from the fabric into the skin of wearers where it is absorbed into the body.

BPA levels in tested socks worn by babies, children and women were from **three times to 19 times above safe levels established by California's Proposition 65**, a safe chemicals law which lists BPA as a danger to the endocrine and reproductive systems of humans. The Center initiated litigation under the law against 95 of the sock brands, including Adidas, Champion, GAP, Hanes, Tommy Hilfiger, New Balance and Reebok.[27]

 **Sweaters**

A team of six scientists from four research centres in China analyzed how micro-plastic fibers in synthetic sweaters release heavy metals as a result of wear. Particularly *high levels of copper and zinc* were found to be leaching from the sweaters manufactured in China and

---

[27] "BPA in Socks: Are There Harmful Chemicals in Your Socks?" Center for Environmental Health, 05/06/22

sold abroad, meaning these metals were being absorbed through the skin of sweater wearers.

Copper is commonly added as complex dyes and potent pro-oxidation catalysts in textiles, whereas zinc is added to sweaters and other textiles as heat stabilisers or part of inorganic dyes. Both metals in small amounts are useful to human health, but prolonged exposure to higher amounts can prove toxic to most organs of the human body.[28]

Garner & Kathryn Nelson surf interview silk/hemp board-short

---

[28] "Leaching of heavy metal from polyester micro-plastic fibers and the potential risks in simulated real-world scenarios." Zuo C. Et al. Journal of Hazardous Materials. 2021 January.

⚜ Swimsuits

A team of toxicologists in Spain tested for heavy metals and other substances in swimsuits sold in Europe to men and women, and children and teenagers of both sexes. High levels of **titanium** turned up in **polyamide fabrics** for swimsuits made to be worn by both sexes, while high levels of **antimony** tested high in **polyester swimsuits** for both sexes, probably due to its use as a catalyst and delustering agent in these synthetic fibers. Dark synthetic swimsuits showed higher concentrations of chromium, aluminium, manganese and magnesium than other colours.

Health risks "could not be calculated due to the lack of information on toxicological data," read the study, but in the case of titanium, "the element with the highest concentrations in swimsuits, and taking into account the potential toxicity of Ti02 nanoparticles {added to swimsuits} further research is need to assess the migration of this element from fibres to skin."[29]

Further research, on the health risks from wearing heavy metals in swim wear, would seem a common sense step to take, since heavy metals have a record of proven toxicity when exposed to human skin over prolonged periods, linked to a range of health hazards, even at low levels of exposure, including neurocognitive impairment, metabolic disorders, cardiovascular and renal diseases, and cancers.

---

[29] "Human exposure to trace elements, aromatic amines and formaldehyde in swimsuits: Assessment of the health risks." Herrero M. Et al. Environmental Research. 2020 February.

Investigation finds evidence of PFAS in workout and yoga pants

Testing finds fluorine—an indicator of PFAS—in women's sportswear from popular brands like Old Navy and Lululemon.

I personally make my own surf board shorts out of my leftover fabric, using hemp and silks. Silk is a natural water repellent and hemp holds up in the action sport of surfing. So far so good! I definitely do not desire to bake my goods in the sun on the beach wearing nylon spandex 4 way stretch board shorts. Spandex (now called Lycra or Lycra Spandex) is made of at least 85% of the polymer polyurethane and several chemicals that are known sensitisers. TDI and MDI (Toluene-2,4-diisocyanate; Methylene bisphenyl-4,4-diiisocyanate) are precursors of the polyurethane used to make spandex. TDI, a toxic chemical, has proved to be carcinogenic and can cause severe dermatitis. MDI is also toxic.

 Workout Wear

A general rule with workout clothes is the more you sweat, the more synthetic chemical toxins you might potentially absorb through your skin, depending on the type of fabric you wear. **It is like smoking while going to the gym.** Underscoring this truism is research, done in 2022 from the "Center for Environmental Health", in which a range of sports bras and workout shirts and shorts were tested for the presence of bisphenol A (BPA), a known hormone-disrupting chemical, commonly added to polyester-based clothing during the manufacturing process to provide anti-static and colourfast properties.

Testing found **BPA to be above safe levels** (as mandated under California's Proposition 65 law) in polyester-based leggings from such companies as *Activ Pro, Amazon Essentials, Outdoor Voices and Wilson*; in polyester-based sports bras by such firms as *Amazon Essentials, Avia, Just Be, Patagonia and Skechers*; in polyester-based athletic shirts from *Activ Pro, Beyond Yoga, Hoka, Outdoor Voices, Patagonia, Under Armour and Xersion*; and in polyester-based athletic shorts from *New Balance, Adidas, Nike, Prana, Asics and Athletic Works*.[30]

Indicators of a class of chemicals called PFAS, (Per-and polyfluoroalkyl substances) added to clothing as a water and stain resistant finish, were reported to be detected via lab tests in women's yoga leggings, workout pants, and sports bras during lab testing commissioned by the safety blog, Mamavation, during 2022.[31]

---

[30] "New Testing Shows High Levels of BPA in Sports Bras and Athletic Shirts." The Center for Environmental Health. October 12, 2022.

[31] "In Depth: First-of-its kind testing points to dangers and unknowns of PFAS in clothing." Elizabeth Gribkoff. *Environmental Health News*. Feb. 15, 2022. https://www.ehn.org/pfas-clothing-2656587709.html

Mamavation reported the 32 pairs of yoga leggings and workout pants, and the 23 sports bras, yielded chemical indicators of PFAS ranging from 284 ppm (parts per million) in LulaRoe leggings, to 58 ppm in Third Love Muse Sports bras, 57 ppm in Adidas Don't Rest Alphaskin Bra, 48 ppm in Champion Freedom Seamless Racerback Sports Bra, 48 ppm in SheFit Sports Bra, to 38 ppm in Nike Women's Medium Support Non-Padded Sports Bra. Other name brands included in the testing survey were UnderArmour, Lane Bryant, and Old Navy.

The huge problem with finding PFAS chemicals in clothing comes from the substances being documented as health hazards, because they persist within human bodies and within the environment. Certain PFAS's are known to alter human metabolism, fertility, reduce fetal growth, advance the risk of becoming overweight or obese, and most dangerously, to increase your risk of cancer.[32]

[32] "Per-and Polyfluoroalkyl Substance Toxicity and Human Health Review: Current State of Knowledge." Fenton SE. Et al. *Environ Toxicol Chem*. 2012 March.

 ## ⚜ Natural Fibers Can be Made Harmful, Synthetics More So

"Although natural fibers, such as cotton and wool, originated from natural sources, they often contain a suite of chemical additives, including colorants (e.g., azo dyes, pigments) and finishes (e.g., flame retardants, antimicrobial agents, ultraviolet light stabilisers). These and other additives --bisphenols, polyfluorinated alkyl compounds (PFAS), and formaldehyde-- are applied to textiles during production to give them desired properties like enhanced durability."[33]

---

[33] "Are We Underestimating Antropogenic Microfiber Pollution? A Critical Review of Occurrence, Methods, and Reporting." Athey SN. Erdle LM. *Environmental Toxicology & Chemistry*. 2021 July.

Chapter IV: The Dark Secret: Toxic Body Burdens Start Skin Deep

 ## Toxins on Skin are More Harmful Than Eating Them

"To varying degrees, **all carcinogens and other toxic ingredients are absorbed through your skin,** directly into your blood, and then circulate all over your body. These ingredients bypass the detoxifying enzymes in your liver that protect you from toxins in food. That means the harmful chemicals that you apply to your skin are much more toxic, and pose greater cancer and other risks, than if you *ate them*"—Dr. Samuel J. Epstein, University of Illinois toxicologist, in *Toxic Beauty*, 2009.

London Fashion Week fittings LTBN collection 2024

Political and commercial interests continue to shape our narrative in fashion for what's healthy for the body to wear. They drive trends, sex appeal, social status, and power in order to mask the chemical toxins that lurk inside each outfit, even when it's proven harmful for our beautiful naked bodies. The human system becomes overloaded with these toxins, the bioaccumulation levels overflowing thus leading to sickness, auto-immune disease, and cancers.

Humorist Mark Twain said it best:

"It ain't what you don't know that gets you into trouble. It's what you know for sure that just ain't so."

Skin Opens the Door to Toxins

Our largest and most vulnerable body organ is our skin, exposing a vast area of ourselves to the absorption of environmental toxins. "Less than one-tenth of an inch thick, skin is a porous and permeable membrane that is highly sensitive to toxic chemicals," wrote Dr. Samuel J. Epstein, a University of Illinois toxicologist and founder of the Cancer Prevention Coalition. "Mainstream manufacturers and regulatory authorities appear unaware of the high permeability of skin, or else simply choose to ignore this as a critical concern."

We interviewed Professor Alison Matthews David, author of the book, *Fashion Victims*, for our documentary and her historical research revealed how hatters were being poisoned by mercury through the cracks in the skin of their hands. This started in 1829, when Paris was at the height of hat production, and a mass epidemic occurred of **acrodynia (pink's disease)** named after the **rashes** it gave over **40,000 Parisians**.

Our skin protects the human body from water loss, harmful microorganisms, irritants, and injuries, and provides an important barrier against exposure to environmental contaminants. Clothes add another barrier, but the direct and prolonged interaction between the *stratum corneum* and the textile material, the latter often synthetic, may be responsible for irritation, sensitization, or even penetration of hazardous chemicals into the human body as a result of leaching from fabrics.

Another study cited in Alison's book, done by Dr. Alexandre Layet, showed that in 1875 in Paris, mercury produced abortions, premature births, and stillbirths in women who worked with toxic pelts as furriers. Alison also told me that she went to the V&A museum for research and the top hat was air tight sealed in cellophane marked by a skull and cross bones only to be touched using gloves.

Evidence that centuries-old poisons still persist in the very fibers of the top hat conflicts with today's industry propaganda trying to reassure us that the harmful chemicals used in clothing production and dye wash out until the fabric is harmless.

Synthetic fabrics such as polyester, nylon, and rayon can restrict your skin from breathing, cause rashes and clog skin pores. As your skin is always in direct contact with fabrics, the type and structure of fabrics can significantly influence the health of your skin. Therefore, it is important to always pay close attention to the type of fabric you wear.

From clothes, undergarments, socks, and towels to bed sheets, switching to healthy fabrics allows your skin to breathe freely, preventing rashes, allergies, and other skin issues that can damage your overall health. Further, the **chemicals from synthetic fabrics can leach through tiny skin pores & hair follicles and settle into your tissue**, thus increasing your bioaccumulation of toxins. I keep telling all of my surf buddies about nylon trucker caps. As we spoke about the synergy of effect when the UV sun rays hit that nylon trucker cap it goes straight into the hair follicles leading to killing those follicles thus loosing hair. A review of 47 articles and studies on alopecia found that heavy metals such as mercury and thallium were the top toxins that caused anagen effluvium. Other heavy metals linked to anagen effluvium include boron, thallium, cadmium, copper and bismuth.

Something else to keep in mind about polyester: It's not just a migration into skin that occurs with the polymers (big repeating chains of molecules) in polyester, but it's also the monomers (the building blocks for polymer molecules) that migrate. During the manufacturing process the monomers get trapped within fibers. Phytoestrogen chemicals (endocrine disrupters) can bind to the polymers and monomers during manufacturing and then be emitted by the polyester into human skin during fabric wear.

Strong Evidence for Toxins Migration

A series of mostly overlooked and under-appreciated science studies about our skin generated findings that should be on the radar of every health conscious person. Here is a representative sampling showing how dangerous toxins migrate through our skin to colonize our bodies:

() Scientists from Sweden and Italy found in 2018 that **benzothiazole**, a contaminant in clothing from garment manufacturing, can "be released from textile materials, penetrate through the skin, and further enter the human body." Greatest harm goes to toddlers who risk developmental and reproductive toxicity over a lifetime from exposure to this chemical leached from clothing.[1]

() Forestry workers wearing permethrin-treated pants were tested in 2019 and shown to have elevated levels of this insecticide (a neurotoxin) in their bodies as a result of skin absorption. The same study found that clothing can absorb other pesticides and transfer it into the homes of farm workers; the herbicide glyphosate, the insecticide malathion, and benzothiazole used in dyes also migrated from fabrics into skin.[2]

---

[1] "Chemicals from textiles to skin: an in vitro permeation study of benzothiazole." Iadaresta F. Et al. Environ Sci Pollut Res Int. 2018.

[2] "Clothing-mediated exposure to chemicals and particles.Licina D. Et al. Environ Sci & Tech. 2019

Advocate Suzy Amis Cameron & Jeff in New Zealand at the interview

() A team of British scientists writing in a 2023 issue of the science journal, *Environmental Science & Technology*, revealed how a class of compounds called brominated flame retardants, added to plastic fibers in clothing fabrics like polyester to prevent burning, migrate into the skin during clothing wear. Sweat also leaches these endocrine system disrupting chemicals from clothing, especially from sports bras and t-shirts, to be absorbed by the skin.[3]

() Brazilian scientists in 2023 tested 240 clothing items sold in Spain and Brazil for the presence of Azo dyes, synthetic dyestuffs used widely in the manufacture of garments. Azo dyes release contaminants called aromatic amines that are absorbed by the skin during wear.

---

[3] "Novel Insights into the Dermal Bioaccessibility and Human Exposure to Brominated Flame Retardant Additives in Microplastics." Abafe OA. Et al. Environ Sci Technol. 2023.

Dozens of types of aromatic amines have been shown to cause cancer. In the 240 garments tested, 75 of them, mostly made of synthetic fibers, contained aromatic amines from the dyes at levels higher than thresholds set as hazards to human health.[4]

Marine Scientist Mark Eriksen from 5 Gyres at his interview

---

[4] "Non-regulated aromatic amines in clothing purchased in Spain and Brazil: Screening-level exposure and health impact assessment." Souza MC. Et al. J Environ Manage. 2023

Our Bodies Act Like Sponges

"The human body is like a sponge for chemicals. We bioaccumulate them in our fat. But once the chemicals enter the body they metabolize. You may ingest one or two compounds and you may end up with five or six more because your body metabolizes and creates new compounds." –Dr. John Laseter, biochemist, quoted in *The Hundred-Year Lie.*

Jeff's logwood bark dye makes purple

A Body Burden of Trojan Horse Toxins

As most people by now know, or at least suspect, each of us is exposed to thousands of synthetic chemicals every day of our lives. Only by doing periodic blood and urine testing, usually as part of government or private science lab group biomonitoring programs, can we identify exactly which chemicals have taken up residence in our body fat and organs.

As part of our documentary, I took a toxicity test with our local Malibu holistic doctor, Dr. Sarah Murphy. As we suspected, I had no traces of toxic metals because I wear my own plant dyed hemp/cotton fabrics. But I did find a detectable concern with Glyphosate, which is a Group 2A carcinogen and used in Round-Up by Monsanto (now Bayer, which use to be a part of the German chemical conglomerate, IG Farben), the most widely used herbicide in the world. I would imagine the connection has to do with my surfing daily at my beach shack in north Malibu. just south of Oxnard where they do a lot of spray pesticide farming. According to a report, County agencies use 1,830 gallons of glyphosate annually on almost 4,400 acres at a cost of roughly $800,000, just to eliminate weeds.

Estimates by the U.S. Centers for Disease Control and Prevention (CDC) and other institutions places the number of chemical residues absorbed into the average person's body at more than 700 chemicals, many of which have been designated as toxic to human and health. Some of these toxins can persist in the body for years without being excreted, a process called bioaccumulation.

One of the first alarming wake-up calls about the extent of our toxic body burden came when the Environmental Working Group (EWG) paid two major laboratories in 2004 to test the umbilical cord blood of 10 children in New York. It had long been thought that *"the placenta shielded cord blood—and the developing baby—from most chemicals and pollutants in the environment,"* observed EWG scientists, but the lab tests revealed 287 different synthetic chemicals in the umbilical cord blood. These included eight perfluorochemicals, used as stain and oil resisters (charactered as likely human carcinogens by the EPA) and dozens of types of brominated flame retardants, also known to be toxic.

Equally disturbing were the implications of this study. (These lab tests cost $10,000 per sample, illustrating why widespread testing for body burden toxins hasn't been more common.) What the lab test results underscored is that a developing child's chemical exposures are greater pound-for-pound than those of adults; and an immature, porous blood-brain barrier allows greater chemical exposures to the developing brain; and body systems that detoxify and excrete chemicals are not fully developed in babies, producing a greater health risk.[5]

---

[5] "Body Burden: The Pollution in Newborns." Environmental Working Group. July 14, 2005.

California initiated a state biomonitoring program in 2012 by testing hundreds of people in its Central Valley region. Results were startling:

() Among 218 persons tested for Bisphenol A (used in the manufacture of fabric polymers) more than **90%** had one or more types of it in their bodies, even though this chemical can cause endocrine disruption, type 2 diabetes, and cardiovascular disease.

() Of 337 persons tested for PFAS (used to make fabrics oil and water repellant) about **99%** of them tested positive for up to four types of PFAS, despite this family of chemicals altering immune and thyroid functions and causing cancer.

() Among 218 persons given blood tests for the presence of phthalates (a plasticizer to print images on garments) **100%** of those tested had up to three types in their bodies, even though these chemicals are known endocrine disrupters.[6]

The grandaddy of all biomonitoring programs remains the CDC's 'National Reports on Human Exposure to Environmental Chemicals,' in which the CDC did testing of blood and urine every few years, between 1999 and 2018, on 2,400 people to assess their body burden of chemicals. Several hundred chemicals, out of more than 80,000 commercial chemicals registered to circulate in the U.S., were

---

[6] "Unweighted Results for the Biomonitoring Exposures Study." Biomonitoring California. 2012. https://biomonitoring.ca.gov/

targeted for the tests. Dozens of the targeted chemicals were detected in every person tested.[7]

Though it may be true that detection doesn't necessarily equal risk, which is the mantra we regularly hear from the CDC and some mainstream toxicologists, we must also temper this attempt at reassurance by taking into consideration several important caveats. For instance, drawing blood is commonly used as the primary means to test for the presence of chemicals in the body. But because "the life span of a red blood cell is only around 90-120 days, past exposures to some chemicals may be underestimated," observed the science journal, *Environmental Health Perspectives*.[8] These toxins live in the fat cells as the body stores them there to avoid contamination as a defence mechanism, which is typically is not being measured.

A second consideration concerns limitations on the scope of testing. No technological method currently exists, nor does the immense funding exist, for lab testing to monitor the more than 85,000 synthetic chemicals registered for circulation in the U.S., or the estimated 350,000 chemicals and mixtures of chemicals circulating commercially worldwide. Only a few hundred chemicals can be searched for at any given time and so the true health perils can only be guessed at.[9]

---

[7] "National Report on Human Exposure to Environmental Chemicals." Centers for Disease Control and Prevention. 2009. https://www.cdc.gov/exposurereport/whats_new_092923_1.html

[8] "Biomonitoring and Biomarkers: Exposure Assessment Will Never Be the Same." Paustenback D. Galbraith D. Environ Health Perspect. 2006 August.

[9] "Toward a global understanding of chemical pollution: a first comprehensive analysis of national and regional chemical inventories." Wang Z. Et al. Environ Sci Technol. 2020.

And finally, but most importantly, a third consideration has to do with the unknown additive and synergistic interactions between the myriad of chemicals lurking in the body. (Additive means when one chemical adds to the health impact of another chemical; synergy means when two or more chemicals interact together to magnify the health impacts beyond what any one chemical can do on its own.)

Darien Olien & Jeff planning the discovery journey for the doc in Malibu

⚜ Synthetic Chemical Interactions Alter Health Rules

"What makes synergy so scary for scientists and government regulators—and even more so for corporate executives—is how it profoundly challenges all traditional risk analysis calculations of whether chemicals in products pose a threat to human health." *--The Hundred-Year Lie*, Randall Fitzgerald, 2007

Dr. Ana Soto in Paris, discussing even low PPMs of chemicals can affect health more

Going back to what I learned in my interview with Alison, men were wearing striped socks in the 1880s that were dyed with Analine dyes and when they would sweat, it would cause a synergy of reaction to the chemicals, as obviously there is salt (sodium chloride) in sweat. Salt is used to produce caustic soda and chlorine, resulting in caustic soda's other name, Sodium Hydroxide, which can cause severe burns and permanent damage to any tissue that comes in contact with it.

I personally have played around with making it using salt, water, aluminum and an electrostatic charge, so you have made caustic soda, something that can happen naturally wearing a sock because of the aluminum in the dye and friction. But yes, the clothing manufacturers did not 'add' caustic soda, only provided one of the ingredients, apparently unknowingly!

It reminds me when I was coming back from Australia after my catwalk shows carrying my wetsuit on my shoulder and going through the airport security scanner. The suit was still wet from my previous surf session before jumping on the plane. Apparently, this new suit had one of the ingredients they look for at airports to make a bomb…so I had to give the wetsuit over to them. That is why my board shorts are hemp & silk and wetsuit in Malibu is natural rubber avoiding those unknown ingredients.

I vote we just do away with toxic harmful cheap ingredients for clothing unless they contain warning labels, including synergy of effect warning labels…as in, please don't sweat in these socks for they will burn you!

Another fun chemistry fact is how in the Scotland Highlands they used to bring guys out of the bar and collect their urine and keep it in a tub for a few weeks, let it ferment, and you got ammonia that was used for a mordant (bind to the cloth) wool dyeing. And in case you're wondering, yes I have used urine for my Indigo dye vats!

That mantra often heard from fashion companies that " *toxin levels in our products are too small to inflict harm"* fails to take into account the role of cumulative impacts from all of the chemicals absorbed taken together, or the resulting chemical synergies and their impact on health. Have you ever gone for a run in your t-shirt and come back with the underarms discoloured? It's a result of the synergy between the aluminum in your deodorant and the heavy metals in the t-shirt's dye, right where your lymph nodes are located.

The clothing industry tries to skirt around regulations restricting formaldehyde, for example, by saying *"We did not add formaldehyde"* to our garments. Yet, formaldehyde, a known carcinogen, can be released by a synergy of other chemicals hidden in the garment. They go by other names, such as:

- Formalin
- Formic aldehyde
- Methanal
- Methyl aldehyde

- Methylene glycol

- Methylene oxide

That's just a glimpse at how easy it is for manufacturers to make it challenging for everyday consumers to avoid carcinogens.

Table 1: Side effects of the chemicals used in the textile fibre manufacture.

Sr. No.	Name of the Chemical used	Name of the Fibre	Side effects on health
1.	Sulphuric acid	Used in manufacturing process of rayon	Can cause skin rashes, itching, redness, dermatitis, necrosis and anorexia
2.	Carbon disulphide	Emitted from rayon fabric	Can cause nausea, headache, vomiting, chest and muscle pain; and insomnia
3.	Nitric acid	Used in rayon	Can produce injuries to the skin, eye, respiratory and gastrointestinal tract
4.	Ethylene glycol	Used in manufacturing of polyester fibre	It can cause dysrhythmias and heart failure
5.	Hexamethylene diamine	Used in manufacturing of nylon fibre	Can irritate skin, eyes, nose, throat and lungs; may also damage the liver and kidneys, infertility in men
6.	Dimethyl formamide	Used in spinning process of acrylic fibre	Causes skin rashes and liver damage
7.	Formaldehyde	Used in spandex, acrylic, nylon and polyester fibres	Causes skin allergies and eye watering
8.	Barium sulphate	Used as antistatic substance in the finishing of polyester, nylon, spandex and acrylic fibres	Causes hyper skin pigmentation, dermatitis, dizziness, headache and spine pain
9.	Terepthalic acid	Used in manufacturing polyester fibre	Carcinogenic
10.	Acrylonitrile	It is used in manufacturing of acrylic fibre	Carcinogenic and has bad effects on central nervous system

 Even at Low Levels, Chemical Combinations Can Harm

"While the government develops safety levels for each chemical separately, in the real world we are exposed to multiple chemicals simultaneously. The synergistic effects of multiple exposures are unknown, but a growing body of research suggests that even at very low levels, the combination of these chemicals can be harmful to our health." *—Margaret Reeves, senior scientist at the Pesticide Action Network.*

The Telegraph

Victoria's Secret sued after bra 'made women ill'

Victoria's Secret, the US lingerie firm, is facing the prospect of being sued by dozens of American women who claim their bras brought them out in painful rashes and welts

By Ben Leach

HEALTH

Thinx settled a lawsuit over chemicals in its period underwear. Here's what to know

JANUARY 19, 2023 · 2:37 PM ET

By Rachel Treisman

 Beware: Synergies from Toxin Interactions

"It is a virtual certainty that other {chemical synergy} effects are occurring in the field that we are presently overlooking in the lab. How can all biodiversity {and human health} be protected from the myriad of chemicals they are now exposed to when we do not even know what is there?" –*Environmental Science & Technology*, 2004

Ā review study in the science journal, *Geohealth*, observed in 2022, how traditional health studies only focus on individual toxins and *"there are relatively few studies on how pollutants mixtures interact,"* and yet it has become clear *"the possibility of synergistic interactions between different pollutants could explain how **even low concentrations can cause major health problems…{including} promote cancer development.**"*[10]

Chemical synergies can no longer be considered a rare occurrence, as the chemical and garment industries continue to claim, declared a review of the evidence in 2023, appearing in the journal, *Current Opinion in Toxicology*. Synergies are being seen during experimental lab studies, even in combinations of low doses, such as those involving such classes of chemicals as pesticides and phthalates, and in endocrine disrupters and carcinogens.[11]

Since there are an almost infinite number of possible real-life mixtures of chemicals to consider as candidates for synergies, both toxicology research and ordinary consumers face the same sort of dilemmas. Complicating factors to consider begin to multiply. **Chemical residues from textiles have the potential to migrate from clothes to the human skin and be absorbed according to their size and octanol/water partition coefficient, and may thus cause local and/or systemic effects.** Harmless compounds or compounds with

[10] "Role of the Synergistic Interactions of Environmental Pollutants in the Development of Cancer." Lagunas-Rangel FA. Et al. Geohealth. 2022 April.

[11] "Synergistic effects of chemical mixtures: How frequent is rare?" Olwenn V. Martin. Current Opinion in Toxicology. 2023.

minor health effect could be metabolized by bacteria present on the skin, or if absorbed, be converted to harmful substances by hepatic enzyme systems. A combination of different toxic compounds could also enhance (or reduce) the health risk of the single substances.

For example, do we start with a person's health condition and work our way back like detectives, trying to figure out chemical exposures? What if the exposures have accumulated from throughout a lifetime? (There is an entire new field of science called **Exposomics** to study how toxic chemicals affect a body over a lifetime.) Or do endless experiments need to be performed on countless chemical combinations to identify the most toxic synergies and then try to link them to the onset of specific health conditions? This could involve generations of research, costing billions of dollars, testing which will need to be continuously updated because the pace of chemical discovery and creation is accelerating.

Three Wildcard Contaminants: Formaldehyde, Azo Dyes, and Microplastics

Formaldehyde, Azo dyes, and microplastics are absorbed by the skin and synergies between them and other toxins can develop, as previously noted, with each of these body contaminants presenting unique challenges to human health.

Formaldehyde Is Everywhere Around Us

Though normally associated in the public's mind with embalming processes, **formaldehyde** has become so ubiquitous in clothing processing because it's inexpensive, readily available, and efficient in making garments more durable. It's easily absorbed by the skin and **it has been labeled a human carcinogen** by the World Health Organization's International Agency for Research on Cancer.[12]

Discovered in 1867, by a German scientist who extracted methanol from the charcoaling of wood, formaldehyde was recognized as a highly toxic chemical early on. But it began to be widely used as a fabric preservative and in mildew resistance, waterproof finishes, the stiffening of nylon, and most importantly, in the setting of dyes to prevent colors from running.

It's a difficult chemical for consumers to avoid because it appears everywhere in the clothing manufacturing process: as a permanent-press wrinkle-proofing agent; as antistatic and anti-shrink finishes to garments; as waterproof finishes; as perspiration-proof finishes; as moth-proof and mildew-resistant finishes; as stiffening for lightweight nylon knits; as a chlorine-resistant finish; and as dyes and printing inks to bind the dyes to fabric fibers. Unfortunately, formaldehyde became a commercial viable chemical used as a disinfectant mass-produced in Germany and the first study of the dangers of this chemical produced in the early 1900s by Martin Fischer

---

[12] "Formaldehyde in Textiles: Technical Bulletin." Cotton Incorporated. 2011.

for the *Journal of the Boston Society for Medical Science.* He subjected animals to formaldehyde gas then studied their lungs with 35 pages of details discovering the highly toxic chemical warning to not inject it anywhere in a living creature or splash it in your eyes!

A scientist who has spent several decades warning the public about the effects of formaldehyde exposure and absorption has been Dr. Ruth A. Etzel, a pediatrician and Professor of Epidemiology at the University of Wisconsin. She is especially concerned with the effects of formaldehyde absorption and inhalation on children and their incidence of asthma and other health conditions in childhood.

In testimony before a U.S. Senate Subcommittee in 2009, Dr. Etzel declared: *"Children may be more susceptible than adults to the respiratory effects of formaldehyde. Even at fairly low concentrations, formaldehyde can produce rapid onset of nose and throat irritation, causing cough, chest pain, shortness of breath, and wheezing. At higher levels of exposure, it can cause significant inflammation of the throat, windpipe and bronchi, inflammation of the lungs, and accumulation of fluid in the lungs."*

She urged Congress to take action that would "limit formaldehyde in children's clothing," noting that "at least a dozen other nations already restrict formaldehyde residues in children's clothing."[13] (See Chapter 5 for more on formaldehyde and human health.)

---

[13] *Killer Clothes: How Seemingly Innocent Clothing Choices Endanger Your Health.* By Anna Maria Clement and Brian R. Clement. The Hippocrates Health Institute. 2011.

Āzo Dyes Migrate Into Skin from Clothing

Āzo's are a class of dyes used to colour synthetic fabrics such as polyester and nylon and acrylic. They are the most abundant and fastest growing category of dyestuffs, with the azobenzene type (referred to as azo dyes) accounting for 70% of dye colorants used annually in worldwide fabric production.

"Ⓜany azo dyes are known to have sensitization, mutagenic and carcinogenic properties," declared a 2021 study in the science journal, *Environmental Pollution*. The six authors of this study tested for azo dyes in a wide range of children's clothing and found 21 different azobenzene disperse dyes in the garments, many of them suspiciously problematic for health, especially given how children are even more susceptible than adults to carcinogens absorbed through skin. [14]

What makes these dyes particularly dangerous is their propensity to release aromatic amines after contact with skin bacteria or after skin absorption and metabolization in the body, a process known as biotransformation. AA's (aromatic amines) are contaminants from the dyes possessing their own nefarious health histories. Many AA's are carcinogens and endocrine disrupters, as proven in lab tests, and may increase the risk of developing breast cancer. When a new, replacement breast cell is created by an older, retiring breast cell, during the replication stage of mitosis, the gene or genes which control the new

---

[14] "Characterizing azobenzene disperse dyes in commercial mixtures and children's polyester clothing." Overdahl KE. Et al. *Environmental Pollution*. 2021 October.

breast cell's length of life and generation of a replacement cell may be mutated by these toxins residing in the adjacent tissues.[15]

Azo dyes releasing 22 known carcinogenic AA's were banned from clothing textiles in the European Union beginning in 2012, but many dozens more remain unregulated and loom as a hazardous chemical of concern for garment wearers. *"Identification of non-regulated aromatic amines of toxicological concern which can be cleaved from azo dyes used in clothing textiles."* Also, *"Azo dyes in clothing textiles can be cleaved into a series of mutagenic aromatic amines which are not regulated yet."*[16]

"Mutagenic AAs in textile azo dyes are of much higher concern than previously expected," warned the scientists who authored a 2017 study of azo dyes in the science journal, *Regulatory Toxicology and Pharmacology*. This shouldn't have come as any surprise because previous studies, several decades ago, had not only shown that azo dyes leach into skin from contact with sweat, but garment manufacturing workers exposed to aromatic amines in the factory had demonstrated increased risks for cancers.

The earliest science evidence for the health dangers of azo dyes appeared in **1956**, when British cancer researchers tested a series of dyes for their effects on mice. Three types of tumours were documented (for the *British Journal of Cancer*) in the mice after exposure to the dyes

---

[15] Ken Smith' Breastcare' Breast Health Facilitator for the American Cancer Society

[16] Bruschweiler BJ. Merlot C. Regulatory Toxicology and Pharmacology. 2017 August.

or their aromatic amines. These dyes were labeled as industrial hazards by the University of Leeds School of Medicine research team. So science and manufacturers have known about these dangers for decades and regulators did nothing to protect chemical workers or consumers.[17]

It's worth noting that during the filming of our documentary this book is based on, we visited Indonesia's Citarum River, home to hundreds of textile factories. The river has become so toxic from textile production chemical residues that it can cause burns on your skin from mere contact. Chemical dyes from these textile plants impacts five million people and the wildlife living in the river basin with life threatening health problems, a result of the river's chemical bath of lead, mercury, arsenic and nonylphenol, all used in the clothes dyeing process. The worst part is that nonylphenol doesn't just poison wildlife, it stays in our clothes even after the garments land on store clothing racks and remains in the fabric leaching out after being washed. Though nonylphenol is banned in the European Union, it remains in use elsewhere in the world.

 ## Microplastics Coat Everything and Everyone

Polyester and other microplastic particles smaller than 4 nanometers can easily penetrate through healthy skin. Even microplastic particles with a size of between 4 and 20 nm can partially

---

[17] "The Induction of Tumours of the Subcutaneous Tissues, Liver and Intestine in the Mouse by Certain Dye-Stuffs and Their Intermediates." Bonser GM. Et al. British Journal of Cancer. 1956 October.

penetrate both healthy and damaged skin, according to research scientists.[18]

Once absorbed through the skin and into the blood, particles are then transported throughout the body, including across the blood-brain membrane barrier. The result can be respiratory and cardiovascular problems and inflammation affecting the central nervous system, contributing to the onset of Alzheimer's and other neurodegenerative diseases.[19]

Eight experts in toxicology from Taiwan published a study in the science journal, *Toxics*, in 2023, featuring a thorough review of science evidence for the origins, absorption, and harmful effects of microplastics on humans and the environment. "There is evidence suggesting that MPs (microplastics) may have negative impacts on different areas of human health," the research team concluded. "These include the respiratory, gastrointestinal, immune, nervous, and reproductive systems, the liver and organs, the skin, and even the placenta and placental barrier."[20]

---

[18] "Do Clothes Make Us Sick? Fashion, Fibers and Human Health." Plastic Soup Foundation, 2022. www.plasticsoupfoundation.org

[19] "Health and Environmental Effects of Particulate Matter." U.S. Environmental Protection Agency, 2022.

[20] "Sources, Degradation, Ingestion and Effects of Microplastics on Humans: A Review." Lin YD. Et al. *Toxics*. 2023 September.

Pioneering research by Dutch scientists in 2022 proved that microplastic particles now dwell in most of our bodies. Blood from 22 healthy adults was analyzed and the results showed that 17 of the volunteers carried a mass of plastic particles concentrated in their bodies.[21]

"No plastic in our water or our bodies" is the mission slogan of The Plastic Soup Foundation, based in The Netherlands, dedicated to research on plastics pollution and the link to human and aquatic life health. Their scientists have documented numerous harmful impacts of health from microplastic absorption, such as:

() Accumulations of microplastics in the body may eventually lead to vascular disease. MPs *"may be neurotoxic, and induce oxidative stress, particularly in the brain and the nervous system."*

() MPs have the property of serving as toxin carriers because highly carcinogenic PAHs are easily absorbed onto MPs. Potential risks exist of getting lung and breast cancer and bladder cancer from exposure of PAHs. Study results show that the most abundant MPs in the placenta, fetal stool, and infant feces were bisphenol A, a known endocrine system disrupter.[22]

---

[21] "Discovery and quantification of plastic particle pollution in human blood." Leslie HA. Et al. *Environmental International*. 2022 May.

[22] "Do Clothes Make Us Sick? Fashion, Fibers and Human Health." Plastic Soup Foundation, 2022. www.plasticsoupfoundation.org

It wasn't until 2004 that someone even coined the term microplastic, though microplastic pollution had been documented starting in 1970, when the oceans were found to be accumulating large amounts of plastic debris, including very small plastic fragments. Microplastics (MPs) "cannot be effectively collected and removed at wastewater stations due to the small particle sizes involved, resulting those plastic particles being discharged into the waters," according to The Plastic Soup Foundation. This fiber release also occurs during the washing of clothes.

Not all MPs end up in the oceans. As the Foundation points out: "Some MPs migrate back to the land from the seas through either the aqueous cycle or the food chain—into animals, plants, and humans. Plants and soil-growing organisms may ingest the plastic particles, followed by their decomposition into MPs, which penetrate deeper into the soil and the food chain through digestion or excretion after ingestion

Amount of microfibres release from laundry shown looks like algae and fish eat it

by living organisms (earthworms, fungi and insects.) The soil's MPs can carry pathogenic bacteria and other pollutants (bisphenols, phthalates, heavy metals, persistent organic pollutants.)"

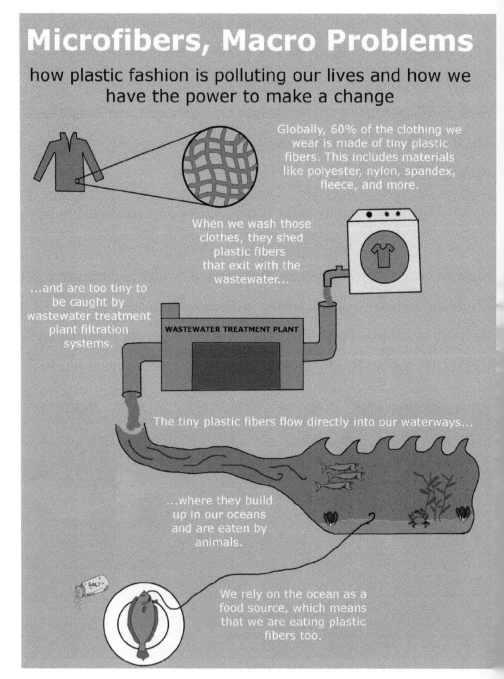

5 Gyres Microfibres Chart

Chemical Contamination Has Become a Wicked Problem

"Over 350,000 anthropogenic chemicals and mixtures of chemicals have been registered for production and use {worldwide} and the myriad of by-products, metabolites and abiotically formed transformation products are not included in this figure. Chemical pollution is therefore a wicked problem characterized by exposure to unintentional complex mixtures found in air, water, soils, food, and household and consumer products." –British Professor of Health and Environment, Olwenn V. Martin, writing in a 2023 issue of the science journal, *Current Opinion in Toxicology*.

The Herald

LUXURY

EDINBURGH

MAY/JUNE 2019

**INTRODUCING
OWNABLE**
The new way to
shop Luxury
Edinburgh

BILL
The
c
ne

**BIG ON
JAPAN**
Your essential
guide to the
Rugby World
Cup host cities

Gown
JEWELS

How American fashion designer Jeff Garner
brought royal style to the Royal Mile

nburgh Castle Catwalk Scottish Linen Gown   Esperanza Spalding Best Dressed for the Oscars

zy Amis Cameron wearing Prophetik gown   Smithsonian Museum Prophetik Pieces

prophetik
wearable philosophy

Chapter V: Profit Before Humanity

 Ā Lot of a Little Still Equals Danger

"We're beginning to realize that the sum total of a person's exposure to all the little amounts of cancerous agents in the environment may be just as harmful as big doses of a few well-known carcinogens. Our chances of getting cancer reflect the full gamut of carcinogens we're exposed to each day—in air, water, and food pollution and in cancerous ingredients or contaminants in household cleaners, clothing, furniture, and the dozens of personal care products many of us use daily." –Dr. Devra Davis, professor of epidemiology, in *Newsweek*, 2007

Garner's redwood beach shack where he lived next door to hippie dad Jim

As Synthetic Clothing Proliferated, So Did Disease

We flew down to West Palm beach to interview the authors of a book called *Killer Clothes* by Anna Maria and Brian R. Clement, PhD, NMD, LN. They have a beautiful holistic health institute called Hippocrates and I needed to experience it firsthand. Any health institute that has a jungle on campus with Iguanas and the cafe serving fresh coconuts outside seems like the right place to receive healing. Hippocrates began by treating cancer with a plant-based diet in the 1950's. One of the interesting things Brian discussed was that, *"Once natural-fiber clothing began to be replaced by synthetics in the 1970s, we started seeing increasing numbers of guests showing up with breast cancer, prostate cancer, and a range of allergic conditions. That trend has accelerated with each passing decade as natural-fiber clothing disappeared from store shelves."* --- Hippocrates Health Institute Co-Directors, Brian & Anna Maria Clement

Hippocrates Institute with Dr. Brian Clement

Maybe it all seems too much…the message that everything seems like it's going to kill you… and so therefore, you decide to just ignorantly enjoy your life without making changes or taking precautions. Let me assure you, as you will learn later in this handbook, there are small yet impactful changes you can make that will counter the accumulation of toxins in your body, leading to a healthier and longer life.

As I explain to all of my friends, the word bioaccumulation, which is in essence the sum of toxins in the body acting out into an allergy, a disease, or cancer. You and I might never smoke and one day, we explore it, and you get lung cancer and I continue smoking for the rest of my life and never get lung cancer. Our body structures are different, my bioaccumulation level could be greater and more tolerable for me, thus maybe I can hold and handle more toxins before triggering health problems. It can be very individualistic and problematic.

That's why in these various scientific studies they find correlations between a specific toxin and a specific health problem, **yet it's not always related to the quantity of toxins absorbed or the exposure time.** We do know it all adds up in the body and results in health problems, some more harmful than others, depending on the person and their physical constitution. The goal is to avoid absorbing and to eradicate as much toxic substances as possible in your everyday life, which for the majority of people comes from the constant contact with clothing worn for majority of hours every day. Our bodies have no mechanism on the skin to protect it from the toxins coming out of the clothing, through the hair follicles, into our blood stream and then into our organs and fatty tissue.

We've shown you in previous chapters how and why everyone carries a 'body burden' of synthetic chemical toxins accumulated from many diverse sources—from our clothing to our food, from our water to our cosmetics and personal care products. Many of these toxins bioaccumulate within our bodies and many were designed to be virtually immortal, never breaking down.

No scientist can even begin to predict when the many hundreds of synthetic chemicals residing in our body fat and organs will reach a tipping point, combining from all sources—clothing, food, water, consumer products, etc.—to eventually trigger health impairment. Given that reality, it makes sense that we should tackle the biggest culprit first… toxins in our everyday clothing.

These x-factors of unpredictability represent largely uncharted territory for government regulators, clothing manufacturers, and the fields of toxicology and medical science. We are left as individuals and as a society with trying to assess each chemical toxin, mostly one at a time, in one article of clothing at a time, and linking them where we can to specific health conditions that have emerged.

The first time that a cancer was diagnosed and linked to a cause seems to have occurred in the late 1700s, when an English surgeon discovered an association between soot exposure and a high incidence of scrotal cancer (a type of squamous cell carcinoma) in chimney sweeps.

It was the first occupational and environmental link to a cancer established in the science literature, showing how skin could transport a toxin. Since that era, of course, finding cause and effect links has become a hallmark of medical science.

Jeff dipping his gown into horse trough logwood dye vat at his farm

When we begin trying to list all or most of the peer-reviewed science studies showing health conditions linked to toxic chemicals in clothing, we find the amount of evidence collected, just over the past few decades, to be so vast as to seem overwhelming. *We can only present a representative sampling in these pages.*

Synthetics Linked to Health Conditions

Breast Health (see a deeper dive later in this chapter)

Cancer (in general)

Disperse dye #1 is used to colour these fabrics: nylon, cellulose acetate and triacetate, polyester and acrylate fibers. This dye has been labeled "reasonably anticipated to be a human carcinogen" by the U.S. Department of Health and Human Services, National Toxicology Program. Animal studies have found it causes urinary-bladder tumours and carcinomas as a result of skin contact. (As of 2009, no commercial manufacturers of disperse blue 1 was identified anywhere worldwide, and yet, five dye suppliers, including three U.S. suppliers, still made it available to fabric makers.)[1]

Ten disperse dyes are classified as carcinogens, meaning repeated exposure may lead to the development cancer, by the European Union's Registration, Evaluation, Authorisation and restriction of Chemicals (REACH) though not by many other countries of the world. The ten are: Disperse yellow 3, Acid red 26, Basic red 9,

---

[1] "Disperse Blue 1. Report on Carcinogens, Fifteenth Edition. National Toxicology Program, U.S. Dept. of Health and Human Services.)

Basic violet 3, Basic violet 14, Direct black 38, Direct blue 6, Direct red 28, Disperse blue 1, Disperse orange 11.[2]

Aromatic Amines (AAs) originate from azo dyes used to treat clothing. AAs are known potential carcinogens. A 2023 study in Brazil measured the urinary levels of AAs in **58 pregnant women, based on their dermal contact with clothes containing azo dyes.** The results showed that **100% of the women had eight types of AAs in their bodies**, two of the AAs regulated by the European Union as cancer hazards. *"AAs have been shown to cross the placental barrier,"* observed the eight study scientists. *"Therefore, prenatal exposure is a significant health concern"* for a variety of adverse birth outcomes. "Assessment of urinary aromatic amines in Brazilian pregnant women and association with DNA damage."[3]

[2] European Commission. REACH Regulation. https://environment.ec.europa.eu/topics/chemicals/reach-regulation_en

[3] Souza MCO. Et al. Environmental Pollution. 2023 October.

Cardiovascular Disease

Microplastic particles have been found embedded in heart tissue, after it being absorbed through the skin, raising the prospect this contamination could trigger cardiovascular disease and a range of heart ailments, such as heart attacks. This discovery was made in 2023 by scientists as a hospital in Beijing, China, when they examined the hearts of 15 patients, between the ages of 40 and 75, after they underwent heart surgery. Nine types of microplastics turned up in five different types of heart tissue and they were found in all blood samples.[4]

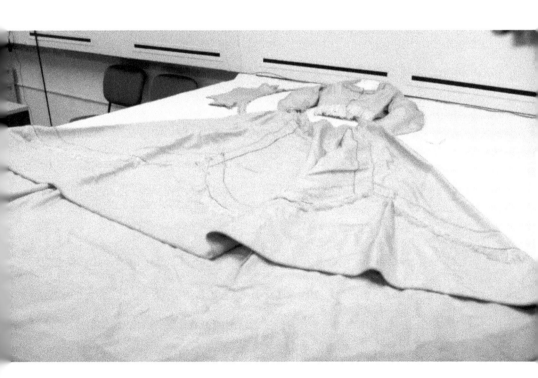

The "green dress" dyed using Arsenic located in Toronto

---

[4] "Detection of Various Microplastics in Patients Undergoing Cardiac Surgery." Yang Y. Et al. *Environmental Science & Technology*. 2023 July.

⚜ Chemical Sensitivities

There is a significant story in history where a woman attended a ball in Paris wearing the latest fashion, an emerald Green Silk Ballgown. She danced the night away with her dance card full as the "nouve' colour brought many wandering eyes to her attention. The next day she died suddenly. Being a noble lady, her family had the gown tested and the amount of **arsenic** in the dress could have **killed 200 men**.

In the book *Fashion Victims*, the author also discussed the **Emerald green scare**, as the powder could release off the gowns and poison others nearby. Yet what stands out as most interesting is that the new emerald colour, being both bold and popular, allowed doctors to actually make a direct connection between the arsenic in the garments worn by the fashionable ladies and to health conditions of the workers who made the gowns and who were being treated for arsenic poisoning. If we could only do that today, more closely correlate cause with toxins in the fabrics, so we could make them illegal.

A second interesting thing is that since the ladies of the houses made the purchasing decisions for the family, they could either listen to the warnings of about wearing the arsenic emerald green dress, or choose to ignore and poison their family. These family decision makers were very productive in stopping this toxic poisoning. They even had popular books in the Victorian era called 'Our domestic poisons'. Doctors, Civil engineers, women's social organized groups, chemists, and media all joined together to vocally stop the use of arsenic in consumer goods. We could learn a thing or two about the **Victorian Arsenic Emerald Green Ballgown Scare.**

Now in our own age, contact dermatitis with problematic eczemas can be triggered by fabrics containing Disperse blue dyes 106 and 124, found in polyester and acetate fibers, often in the liners of women's clothing, or in dress clothing (polyester, acetate and nylon) and dark-coloured nylon stockings, also in children's diapers. "Disperse blue dyes 106 and 124 are common causes of textile dermatitis."[5]

Another great story that Alison, author of *Fashion Victims*, told me during the interview we did together in Toronto, concerned a gentleman who bought a new pair of canvas shoes before going to a dance. He dyed the light canvas tops with a liquid black polish and unfortunately, he had to wear them wet in order to make the dance on time. He filled a bunch of dance cards that evening and following the party he went with his mates to a bar and soon fell ill. His mates placed him in a carriage home thinking him merely over-served with alcohol, but unfortunately, he died five hours later. It was discovered in the autopsy that the shoe polish contained **nitrobenzene,** which is **also used in clothing dyes**.

For those that don't know, nitrobenzene treated with fuming nitric acid is known in the chemical industry as the most dangerous process, a cheap but dangerous solvent also used in **dry cleaning, nail**

5 Pratt M. Taraska V. *American Journal of Contact Dermatitis.* 2000 March. And, "Where is disperse blue mix 124/106 found? Contact Dermatitis Institute, Allergen Database. www.contactdermatitisinstitute.com

polish, glues, and detergents! Listed as a **group 2 Carcinogen,** the oil is readily absorbed by the skin, according to the EPA. If you smell almonds, I say start running as **the chemical oxidizes iron in the blood**. History teaches us that we should not ignore such stories because this chemical gets used throughout the clothing industry, creating serious health effects for clothing workers and garment wearers. It is still happening today. There are many other historical deaths from dyes that Alison covers in her book, *Fashion Victims*, if one is interested for more toxic sad stories.

We show in the documentary Alison's amazing research of photos of the skin eruptions from gloves, socks, stockings, etc., taken from the St. John's Hospital for skin diseases in London. A lot of great brands were built out of necessity during this time, one being **Jaeger** socks. Gustav Jaeger was a German botanist and hygienist who believed that everyone should wear un-dyed wool. He based it off a story of a lady who went dancing and got open sores on her feet. The dyes went straight into her blood stream, poisoning her, and doctors had to amputate both feet!

Jockey underwear is another one born out of necessity in the U.S. in 1867. The lumber jacks in Wisconsin were losing their feet from frostbite, so they developed the thick wool sock to keep them safe. They also developed the first men's brief out of wool in 1937. Still family owned today, I believe the company would be one of the first large commercial manufacturers to shift their production back to natural fibers and dyes, if the consumers demanded it. I have met with them several times in their headquarters in Kenosha, Wisconsin. They had to move their manufacturing overseas in order to compete but would be anxious to get it back and employ more people in their town.

In my Tennessee hometown is a man called **Colonel Littleton**, who went to school with my mom at Lipscomb University. He now employs half the town to make his accessory goods that last forever, probably the best quality production I've seen in a long time. He pays the employees well, they are treated like family, and he consciously chose to keep the town alive, versus producing cheaper overseas. He provides a clear example of how it can be done for local fair trade quality craftsmanship to thrive.

'Beyond the Forest' Collection shot in Tennessee, Jeff's gown handmade Dupioni silk, hemp bodice

Formaldehyde is widely accepted to be a sensitizer, an allergen capable of triggering allergic reactions (and cancer in high doses). Also classified by the EPA as class B1, probably carcinogen, meaning it has been linked with an increase of cancer. Spanish scientists tested 122 synthetic and cotton clothing items from the European market, worn by pregnant women, babies and toddlers, in 2022, and found **one out of every five garment contained formaldehyde**. The highest levels were measured in women's jeans, leggings and panties, and in toddler's trousers. Two pairs of black panties had the highest formaldehyde levels of all--- both were made of 100% organic cotton.[6]

I must note in the study above how 25 of these samples had "official" certification. OKEO-TEX allows garments to pass with Formaldehyde levels which I think are ludicrous, whereas GOTS certified allows none. The study found quantifiable amounts of the toxin in some garments, to negate the certification in a way that shows

[6] "Early-Life Exposure to Formaldehyde through Clothing." Herrero M. Et al. *Toxics*. 2022 June.

there is an issue. Government agencies, certification programs, and manufacturers regard these cases and tests as percentages, but I see them differently because I have a 0% tolerance for cancer causing chemicals.

Formaldehyde was researched by the U.S. FDA in regards to hair straighteners in early 2000s, when it became popular. Salons had issues and health concerns. According to the FDA website, "These products often contain **formaldehyde**, also known as **formalin and methylene glycol**. When the solution is heated, the formaldehyde in the products is released into the air as a gas. Formaldehyde is a colourless, strong-smelling gas that presents a health hazard when breathed into the lungs, or when it gets into the eyes or **onto the skin**. According to the National Cancer Institute, when formaldehyde is present in the air at levels exceeding 0.1 ppm, some individuals may experience adverse effects such as watery eyes; burning sensations in the eyes, nose, and throat, coughing, wheezing, nausea, and skin irritation. Every time I get in a new car I immediately have these effects that "new" car smell is full of formaldehyde off gassing. In our documentary we used a thermal camera to capture this off gassing showing the polyester cloth seats holding a temperature around 105 on a 60 degree day in the shade. The new car even had a prop 65 sticker on the windshield saying it has chemicals that are known to cause cancer. Some people are very sensitive to formaldehyde, whereas others have no reaction to the same level of exposure. "**Formaldehyde** has also been **classified as a human carcinogen** by the International Agency for Research on Cancer."

Again, this supports the argument that even 0.1 ppm of formaldehyde can have a negative effect on an individual.

From the Occupational Safety and Health Administration,

*"Workers can inhale formaldehyde as a gas or vapour or **absorb it through the skin** as a liquid. They can be exposed during the treatment of textiles and the production of resins. The permissible exposure limit (PEL) for formaldehyde in the workplace is 0.75 parts formaldehyde per million parts of air (0.75 ppm) measured as an 8-hour time-weighted average (TWA). The standard includes a second PEL in the form of a short-term exposure limit (STEL) of 2 ppm which is the maximum exposure allowed during a 15-minute period."*

When I mention formaldehyde in my talks, everyone's first reaction is to ask don't they use that in funeral homes? In a cohort study, which simply means a group of researchers followed a group exposed to a certain chemical (formaldehyde) to see if they develop disease over time, funeral industry workers who had died between 1960 and 1986, were compared to those who had died from hematopietic and lymphatic cancers and brain tumours. Haematological cancers such as leukaemia develop in the blood or bone morrow. Lymphatic cancers develop in the tissues and organs that produce, store, and carry white blood cells that fight infections and other diseases. This study analysis showed that those who had performed the most embalming and those with the highest estimated formaldehyde exposure had the greatest risk of myeloid leukaemia. Since then, cancer investigators have concluded that exposure to formaldehyde may cause leukaemia, particularly myeloid leukaemia, in humans. So once again, I wonder why we are still using formaldehyde in textiles?

As with most toxic substances, since consumers can't all be chemists, we do not know the various names of these chemicals or the synergy of chemicals that can create more toxic ones. It's a dirty secret how the industry tries to escape accountability simply by saying "No toxic chemical was added," or our products are "free of formaldehyde".

Below is what's currently explained on the Victoria Secrets website, but it lacks authoritative references and as we have pointed out, on published reviewed studies, what they say is inaccurate and misleading. They attempt to normalize formaldehyde by saying it appears in a lot of products, giving us constant exposures. Strangely a lot of the Victoria Secrets lace bras are made of nylon, which uses caustic soda, chloroform, sulphuric acid, and formaldehyde during its manufacturing. So maybe it wasn't added to the final product but it was manufactured with formaldehyde if the fabric is nylon! Having any carcinogenic fabric on your breasts all day cannot be good and as we have learned, certain chemicals react with little ppms, versus a lot, is just like smothering a fire with too much wood.

Here is how Victoria Secret rationalizes their position:

"Formaldehyde is found naturally in the environment and is widely used in many consumer products. You could expect to find it in dollar bills, medicines, wood furniture, baby wipes ... even fresh fruit and vegetables. Although formaldehyde is quite common, we do not add it to

any of our bras simply because there's no need to use it in this type of product. The most stringent textile guidelines in the world also take into account that there is often formaldehyde found in the environment that make a true zero test result nearly impossible."

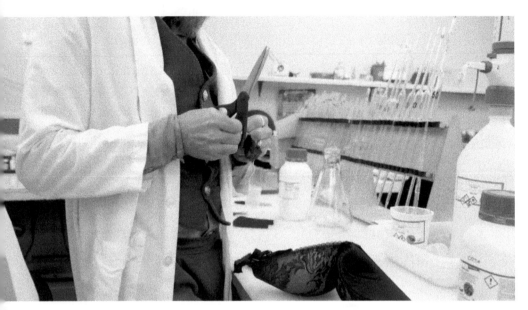

Jeff cutting up a Nylon lace bra with foam at the testing lab to test

According to scientific literature, any level of formaldehyde less than 16 parts per million (ppm) is considered to be "non-detectable," "non-existent" or a "false positive" reading. Dermatologists indicate that even those individuals who are allergic to formaldehyde would not have a reaction at this low level. The Victoria's Secret bras that we tested all had formaldehyde levels below 16 ppm — well below the accepted standard for adult clothing in direct contact with skin, which is 75 ppm.

We did however, find another toxic ingredient above the legal limit in PPMs which you see below highlighted called Nonylphenol (NP) known as a endocrine disruptor, an xenoestrogen, and associated with breast cancer. So it shows that one needs to know the makeup of something in order to test appropriately.

Test result:

Sample	Detected substances in mg/kg	Sum BP + NP + OP + HpP + PeP in mg/kg	Sum BP + NP + OP + HpP + PeP + NP(EO)$_{1-20}$ + OP(EO)$_{1-20}$ in mg/kg
Composite sample:			
1 Woven fabric, Purple Ribbed: 53 % polyester/44 % nylon/ 3 % spandex	NP(EO)$_{1-20}$: 4,4	n.d.	4,4
2 Woven fabric, Grey: 65% polyester/31% rayon/ 4 % spandex			
3.1 Knitted fabric, colour skin	NP(EO)$_{1-20}$: 225 NP: 12,0	**12,0**	237
3.2 Foam, colour yellow	NP(EO)$_{1-20}$: 49,2 NP: 35,2	**35,2**	84,4
Limit values acc. appendix 4			
Product classes I-IV	Σ (BP + NP + OP + HpP + PeP)		< 10 mg/kg
	Σ (BP + NP + OP + HpP + PeP + NP(EO)$_{1-20}$ + OP(EO)$_{1-20}$)		< 100 mg/kg
Limit of quantitation	4,00 mg/kg		
Note	n.d. = not detectable		

(A copy of our test results from the bra highlighted)

In response to the question of whether they add formaldehyde, *"No. We do not add formaldehyde to our bras, and multiple independent tests have confirmed that the bras are formaldehyde-free or contain only trace amounts which are significantly lower than allowed by the most stringent textile guidelines in the world."*

Formaldehyde can be listed on a product label by many other names, such as:

- Formalin
- Formic aldehyde
- Methanal
- Methyl aldehyde
- Methylene glycol
- Methylene oxide
-

Some chemicals that are used as preservatives can release

formaldehyde, such as:

- Benzylhemiformal
- 2-bromo-2-nitropropane-1,3-diol
- 5-bromo-5-nitro-1,3-dioxane
- Diazolidinyl urea
- 1,3-dimethylol-5,5-dimethylhydantoin (or DMDM hydantoin)
- Imidazolidinyl urea
- Sodium hydroxymethylglycinate
- Quaternium-15

Dementia

(Microplastics accumulate in human tissue and as a result, these particles shed from clothing and other sources show the capability of changing behaviour in humans, even triggering dementia. To test this idea a team of scientists studied the neurological effects and inflammatory response to microplastics in the bodies of mice. It was found that microplastic exposure resulted in the particles collecting in every body organ of the mice, including their brains. It had long been thought these particles couldn't penetrate the blood-brain barrier of mammals, but this idea turned out to be deeply wrong. With increasing exposure to microplastics the lab animals began behaving strangely, showing signs of dementia. These symptoms were most pronounced in the older animals, giving a strong inference this might also be happening in older humans.[7]

Endocrine Disruption

Heavy metal exposure has been linked to endocrine (hormone) system disruption, especially in pregnant women and in their children. A team of 9 scientists in Spain conducted a study in 2023 in which they analyzed heavy metal elements found in 120 clothing items sold in that country, including many garments for pregnant women and infants. Aluminium, zinc, and titanium showed the highest concentrations in the most clothes, and chromium (used in synthetic fiber dyes) was similarly detected widely. The highest health risk was found for titanium which is

---

[7] "Acute Exposure to Microplastics Induced Changes in Behaviour and Inflammation in Young and Old Mice." Gaspar L. Et al. *International Journal of Molecular Science*. 2023.

found regularly in synthetic fiber clothing. Early life exposure to these metals through a mother's exposure, noted the scientists, *"has been associated with preterm birth and impaired fetal growth."*[8]

Using flame retardants in clothing fibers "are associated with adverse health effects in animals and humans," wrote ten scientists in the science journal, *Reviews on Environmental Health.* These health impacts include "endocrine and thyroid disruption, immunotoxicity, reproductive toxicity, cancer, and adverse effects on fetal and child development and neurologic functions."[9]

An entire range of endocrine disrupting chemicals can be found in synthetic clothing. These chemicals can disrupt many different hormones resulting in diabetes, obesity, cardiovascular problems, certain cancers, neurological and learning disabilities, etc. As we previously pointed out, one of the most concerning are a family of over 4,500 chemical compounds called per- and polyfluoroalkyl substances (PFAS) used to give clothing grease and water-repelling properties. These chemicals persist and bioaccumulate in human and animal bodies (giving them the nickname 'forever chemicals) and they can survive in the environment for generations.

We also need to talk about the TDI found in almost every stretch garment, TDI being a major hormone disrupter. I see young beautiful surfer girls working at Sunlife Organics in malibu drinking shakes and

---

[8] "Clothing as a potential exposure source of trace elements during early life." Herrero M. Et al. *Environmental Research.* 2023 September.

[9] "Halogenated Flame Retardants: Do the Fire Safety Benefits Justify the Risks?" Shaw SD. Et al. Reviews on Environmental Health. 2010.

wearing my worst nightmare, Lulu Lemon or some other tight fighting lycra polyester-based yoga pant. I look closely and see on the back of their neck and shoulders tiny bumps from their skin breaking out from contact with these hormone disruptors because they wear these pants tightly close to their skin, sometimes without undergarments, all day long and even go work out in them and sweat. We know these toxins penetrate through the hair follicles and sweat glands into the body. The industry continues to want you to believe there is no linkage, but in my opinion all you need to do is to look around you.

Spandex (now called Lycra or Lycra Spandex), introduced in 1958, is a synthetic fiber made of at least 85% of the polymer polyurethane. Spandex is made from several chemicals that are known sensitizers--- TDI and MDI (Toluene-2,4-diisocyanate; Methylene bisphenyl-4,4-diiisocyanate) that are precursors of the polyurethane used to make spandex. TDI, a toxic chemical, has proved carcinogenic and can cause severe dermatitis.

Fertility/Reproduction Disorders

Reproductive epidemiologist Dr. Shanna H. Swan caused a furor in 2017 when she published a science paper detailing how male sperm counts had fallen more than 50 percent in the previous 40 years. She put the blame on the proliferation of endocrine-disrupting synthetic chemicals. Her research was updated in 2023, with the finding that the world-wide decline in sperm count and quality is not only continuing, its' accelerating! Every continent on the planet sees this disruption of male reproductive health.[10]

Clues about possible causes of this reproductive decline have been showing up in the science literature for decades in both human and animal studies. A 2017 animal study, for instance, showed how silver nanoparticles (used in clothing fabrics) were absorbed by skin and cells and produced testicular and sperm toxicity in males and ovarian and embryonic toxicity in females. Exposure to these nanoparticles impaired development and cognitive behaviour in the offspring of females.[11]

A pioneer researcher in the realm of male infertility was the late Professor Ahmed Shafik with the Faculty of Medicine at Cairo University in Egypt. He published around 500 studies in the early 1990s demonstrating how synthetic clothes, particularly **polyester underwear, could cause infertility and diminished sexual function**. In one study, 14 men wore a polyester sling around their scrotums for 12 months, and all of them experienced decreases in testicular volume and had 'contraceptive' effects---they were unable to get their wives pregnant.[12]

---

[10] "Temporal trends in sperm count: a systematic review and meta-regression analysis of samples collected globally in the 20th and 21st centuries." Levine H. Et al. *Human Reproduction Update*. 2023.

[11] "A review of reproductive and developmental toxicity of silver nanoparticles in laboratory animals." Ema M. Et al. *Reproductive Toxicology*. 2017 January.

[12] "Contraceptive efficacy of polyester-induced azoospermia in normal men." Shafik A. *Contraception*. 1992 May.

A second Shafik study used 24 male dogs divided into two groups—the first wore cotton underpants, the second wore polyester. After 24 months, examinations revealed a significant decrease in sperm count and motile sperm in the dogs wearing polyester, but no such effects in the cotton group.[13]

Finally, my favorite study about the linkage of polyester boxers to male impotence! Professor Ahmed took 75 rats, splitting them into 5 groups, including one control and four groups wearing 100% cotton, 100% wool, 100% polyester or a 50:50 poly-cotton mix underwear. Their sexual behaviour was assessed after 6 and 12 months of wearing the garments and 6 months after removing them.

All groups (apart from the control) showed a more marked reduction in "intromission to mounting ratio" after 12 rather than 6 months. At 6 months there was no notable difference in the cotton and wool wearing rats. The 100% polyester group showed the highest reduction followed by the polyester-cotton mix. Six months after removing the underwear all groups returned to normal. It was thought that the electrostatic fields generated in the intra-penile structures could explain the reduced sexual activity.

As a kid did you ever run across the carpet and shock one of your friends? That is the electrostatic discharge coming from the polyester carpet traveling through you. Imagine what that would do to a men's scrotum? Polyester is hydrophobic in nature, not allowing moisture to

---

[13] "Effect of different types of textile fabric on spermatogenesis: an experimental study." Shafik A. *Urology Research*. 1993.

pass, and therefore creating electrostatic discharges, one gateway to infertility.

Tin compounds are sometimes used in garments to prevent body odor from accumulating in fabric. European Union regulations forbid two types of organotin (tin) compounds (Tributyltin and dioctyltin) at levels above 0.1% in clothing, though most other countries don't have such regulations. Studies have shown these compounds can alter human immune and reproductive systems.[14]

Female infertility has been linked to the absorption of PFOAs, a PFAS chemical used in clothing to add stain resistance. Blood levels of PFOA and a related chemical, PFOS, were measured at weeks 4-14 of pregnancy among 1,240 women in Denmark. A science team discovered that women with the highest levels of these chemicals in their bodies increased their likelihood of infertility by up to 154 percent compared to women with the lowest levels of the chemicals. Those with the highest levels also had more irregular menstrual cycles.[15]

---

[14] "Organotin compounds." Allergystandards.com/news_events/chemicals-in-textiles-and-the-health-implications/ Ireland.

[15] "Maternal levels of perfluorinated chemicals and subfecundity." Fei C. Et al. *Human Reproduction*. 2009 May.

Gastrointestinal Disorders

Irritable Bowel Disease: Researchers examined stool samples of patients with *irritable bowel disease* and found "that concentrations of fecal microfibres positively correlated with disease severity of two types of IBD (Crohn's disease and ulcerative colitis.) Triggering particularly severe symptoms were nylon fibers apparently shed from synthetic textiles.[16]

Microplastic fibers were linked to inflammatory bowel disease in a 2023 study in the science journal, *Environmental Research*. "The incidence of inflammatory bowel disease has been increasing in recent years," noted the four study authors. "Our systematic analysis of in vitro and in vivo studies found that MPs (microplastics) induce intestinal barrier dysfunction, imbalance in the intestinal microbiome, and metabolic abnormalities, ultimately leading to Inflammatory Bowel Disease."[17]

Polyester fibers are usually contaminated by antimony (a heavy metal) because it's used as a flame retardant synergist in polymer production for textiles. Exposure to antimony can cause gastrointestinal problems such as stomach ulcers and pancreatitis. One form of it, antimony trioxide, is a suspected carcinogen for humans. And yet,

---

[16] "Analysis of Microplastics in Human Feces Reveals a Correlation between Fecal Microplastics and Inflammatory Bowel Disease Status." Yan Z. Et al. *Environmental Science & Technology*. 2022.

[17] "Effects of microplastics in aquatic environments on inflammatory bowel disease." Ji J. Et al. Environmental Research. 2023 July.

"there is no regulatory limit on antimony concentrations in polyester apparel," according to a 2021 study.[18]

"There is a clear relationship between high exposure to microplastic fibers (nylon) and two types of irritable bowel disease IDB: Crohn's disease and ulcerative colitis."[19]

 Inflammation (chronic)

"Once inhaled, synthetic fibers can penetrate in the lung tissue. As a response, important cells in the immune system, so-called dendritic cells and macrophages, will engulf the plastic particles. Macrophages have the machinery to break down bacteria, but they lack the tools to break down plastic particles. They do try but fail, and keep trying. This process will cause chronic inflammation…known to be a leading cause of diseases such as cancer, heart disease, asthma, and diabetes."[20]

This study really hit home for me. When I began my career in fashion, working for my music artists friends out of Nashville, my sample maker became sick. She had spent 20 years cutting synthetic

[18] "Antimony release from polyester textiles by artificial sweat solutions: A call for a standardized procedure." Biver M. Et al. *Regulatory Toxicology and Pharmacology.* 2021 February. Also, "Antimony: Overview." The National Institute for Occupational Safety and Health. www.cdc.gov/niosh/topics/antimony/default.html

[19] "Do Clothes Make Us Sick? Fashion, Fibers and Human Health." Plastic Soup Foundation, 2022. www.plasticsoupfoundation.org

[20] "Microplastic and nano-plastic transfer, accumulation, and toxicity in humans." Stapleton, PA. *Current Opinion in Toxicology.* 2021.

fabric without a mask and cut microfibres had entered her nose into her lungs.

These studies don't give you a sense of how many garment workers throughout the world we've lost due to using these nasty cheap toxic ingredients they are exposed to. Generally, the workers are unaware of the dangers, so they have no choice. In general the workers get no warnings, and no one making sure they are wearing safety gear. This is an ethical issue, a human rights issue, a moral issue.

Microplastics from synthetic clothing fibers, as well as other sources, can cause several types of toxicity in the human body. Absorbing these tiny pieces of plastic can cause "inflammatory lesions…and the inability of the immune system to remove synthetic particles may lead to chronic inflammation and an increase risk for neoplasia {uncontrolled growth of cells that become cancerous}," a five -person science team concluded in 2020. "Furthermore, microplastics may release their constituents, absorbed contaminants and pathogenic organisms" to further contaminate the human body.[21]

⚜ Lung Diseases

"Airborne microplastics could seriously harm human immune health. Synthetic fibers can penetrate deep into the lung. Both cellulosic and plastic microfibres were found in lung tissue taken from patients

---

[21] "Environmental exposure to microplastics: An overview on possible human health effects." Prata JC. Et al. *Science of The Total Environment*. 2020 February.

with different types of lung cancer. Lung tissue of these diseased patients was studied with a microscope and 97% of the specimen contained fibers." [22]

We filmed this in our documentary, but I want everyone to connect the dots. Think about that new car you just bought and its new car smell…what do you think those seats are made of? Polyester sprayed with some gnarly chemical to make it stain resistant? The answer most likely is yes…and what about fake leather or let's call it vegan leather…or better yet vinyl. You probably saw footage of that train wreck derailment in Ohio carrying vinyl chloride that once it burns it forms dioxins. Vinyl chloride causes angiosarcoma of the liver, a rare but extremely dangerous form of liver cancer. Do we believe it is safe or changes its molecular structure to no longer be a danger to us once used to form a plastic product? The answer is no…it leaches and off gases…so the world was brought to attention with the train wreck… now it is time to stop using these chemicals and learn from our history.

Dr. Phoebe Stapleton of Rutgers University "exposed pregnant rats to airborne nano-plastics and then determined the amount of plastic in tissue of both mother and unborn rats. She concluded that nano-plastic particles transferred to unborn rats within 9 hours {of mother's exposure}. Plastic was not only found in the lungs of pregnant rats, but also in liver, lungs, heart, kidneys and brain of unborn rats {in the womb}."[23]

 ## Neurodegenerative Diseases

In a 2022 study in the *International Journal of Environmental Research and Public Health* a team of scientists revealed results for heavy metals found in 14 mostly synthetic clothing items manufactured in the Czech Republic, Spain, Germany, Romania and Bangladesh. High levels of chromium and manganese were measured in socks, manganese and titanium in cycling pants, and barium in long sleeve shirts. Concentrations of the carcinogens arsenic, mercury and lead appeared in several garments and far exceeded European regulations. These metals were either contaminants, or they were secretly used in various phases of the clothing manufacturing processes. Heavy metal exposure has been linked to neurodegenerative diseases such as Alzheimer's and Parkinson's.[24]

---

[23] "Microplastic and nano-plastic transfer, accumulation, and toxicity in humans." Stapleton, PA. *Current Opinion in Toxicology.* 2021.

[24] "Metal Content in Textile and (Nano) Textile Products." Rujido-Santos I. Et al. Int J Environ Res Public Health. 2022 January.

A previous study of heavy metal content in clothing fibers manufactured in Turkey (but sold internationally) made similar discoveries. Both synthetic and cotton textile fibers of different colours were collected from numerous manufacturing plants and subjected to several analytical techniques. *"Iron and aluminium were detected in the highest concentrations in all examined textile fibers,"* reported the science team. *"The levels of cadmium and lead in all examined textile fibers were found considerably higher than the value demanded by Oeko-Tex {a textile safety certification}."*[25]

Let's discuss for a moment Oeko-Tex and the other fabric certification brands whose names are being mentioned. When I first started in sustainable fashion, there were no such certifications back in 2000. A book called *Cradle to Cradle by Michael Braungart and William McDonough* had just been published and it became the newest rage and soon thereafter, these 'standards' or certification programs began. I never quite understood them, as I was already doing things naturally, all by myself. Why would I pay someone to place their logo on my product when I was already making something better without their certification.

Then I realized in my opinion it was a money-making deal. They claimed that with their logo I would be able to sell more of my product and they would help advertise my products. But they could not explain to me how they actually certified the efficacy of what I was

---

[25] "Determination of Metal Contents of Various Fibers Used in Textile Industry by MP-AES." Sungar S. Et al. *Hindawi*. 2015.

producing. There was no testing involved you just filled out this form… again, self-regulated, which meant that people could manipulate truth and labels for their benefit.

So no thank you, I would rather stick to my own accountability process and good intentions. But we will get into this deeper later, in Chapter 7, about what to look for and why not to trust a label or certification. Since it is your only body, you need to police what you place on it and not get manipulated by misleading certification labels.

Obesity/Weight Gain

"Something strange is going on," declared scientists at the Plastic Soup Foundation. *"The average intake of calories in the United States has remained stable or has even dropped over the last 20 years, while the percentage of people suffering from obesity has risen from 30.5% to 42.4% How can this be explained?"*

The answer seems to be that **fat formation is being stimulated by exposure to microplastics and the additives they carry, because these are obesogens**, a term to describe chemicals that help to make humans gain weight.[26]

Obesogen chemicals in synthetic clothes fibers include **bisphenol A**, certain phthalates, organophosphate flame retardants, the various PFASs and a range of other endocrine disrupters, according to

---

[26] "Chemicals Plastic Cause Overweight." www.plasticsoupfoundation.org February 14, 2022.

the science journal, *Chemistry World*. At least 50 product chemicals and classes of chemicals, probably more, **literally make humans fatter**.[27]

A team of 21 scientists, writing in a 2022 issue of *Biochemical Pharmacology,* examined the science evidence and came to these conclusions: the most sensitive time for exposure to fat-producing obesogens is in the womb and early childhood and this exposure, through epigenetic programming, can be transmitted to future generations, further fueling the obesity epidemic; and these obesogen chemicals *"can act at very low concentrations,"* meaning almost no level of exposure is completely safe; and these chemicals impact type 2 diabetes, non-alcoholic fatty liver disease, insulin resistance and hormone disruption.[28]

 Prostate Health

High levels of bisphenol A (BPA), a notorious endocrine (hormone) disrupter, turned up in socks, sports bras, and athletic shirts, all polyester/spandex blends, analyzed by scientists at the Center for Environmental Health. **About 100 clothing companies**, including famous ones like Adidas and Hanes, **were caught using toxic levels of bisphenol in manufacturing their products.** (Socks contained up to 31 times the legal limit under California's chemical harm laws.)[29]

---

[27] "Are everyday chemicals contributing to global obesity?" Chemistry World. December 19, 2022.

[28] "Obesity II: Establishing causal links between chemicals exposures and obesity." Heindel J. Et al. *Biochemical Pharmacology*. 2022 May.

[29] "What You Need to Know About BPA in Clothing." Center for Environmental Health. https://ceh.org/what-you-need-to-know-about-bpa-in-clothing. February 24, 2023.

BPA mimics the hormone, oestrogen, and in men its effects can be severely disruptive to normal functioning of the prostate gland. *"We found a higher risk of prostate cancer for the increase in serum BPA levels,"* reported scientists in Spain who examined 575 prostate cancer cases. Similar evidence from BPA exposure was found in lab animal models.[30]

Another potential trigger for the onset of prostate cancer comes from the chemicals used in the clothes dye process. The starting point in the **production of most dyes begins with benzene, toluene and xylene.** These three chemicals have been identified as carcinogens and some studies have **linked them to a greater risk for the onset of an aggressive form of prostate cancer.** [31]

---

[30] "Bisphenol-A exposure and risk of breast and prostate cancer in the Spanish European Prospective Investigation into Cancer and Nutrition study." Fernandez ES. Et al. *Environmental Health.* 2021 August.

[31] "Four common workplace substances linked to prostate cancer." Industrial Safety & Hygiene News. August 2, 2018. Also, "Assessing volatile organic compounds exposure and prostate-specific antigen: National Health and Nutrition Examination Survey, 2001-2010." Wei Ch. Et al. Front Public Health. 2022.

Thyroid Disease

By measuring the levels of PFOA and PFOS concentrations in the blood of 3,974 adults and comparing those results to the incidence of thyroid disease, scientists were able to draw several inferences. (Both PFOA and PFOS are chemicals used in clothing for stain resistance.) Those persons with the highest concentrations of the chemicals in their book were twice as likely to develop thyroid disease as those with lower concentrations. These results find support in animal studies where hormone imbalances occurred after contact with the two chemicals.[32]

A Deeper Dive: Bras and Breast Health

California community newspaper editor and columnist Debra DeAngelo sounded a personal alarm about bras and breast health in a May 2013 blog post:

"So, I started to itch, uncontrollably. I've heard of jock itch. But breast itch? Could there be so such a thing? All I know is that mine started itching wickedly. We're talking chicken pox covered in poison oak itchy. You can't NOT scratch. Even to the point of bruising.

No joke.

---

[32] "Association between Serum Perfluorooctanoic Acid (PFOA) and Thyroid Disease in the U.S. National Health and Nutrition Examination Survey." Melzer D. Et al. *Environmental Health Perspectives.* 2010 January.

It was that bad, and I scratched myself raw. And it wasn't the first time this had happened, but it was mostly definitely the worst. I was covered in welts, red everywhere and miserable. My skin was dry and papery, particularly on the nipples."

A clue to what was happening came when Debra washed and dried the Victoria's Secret all-cotton heather gray bra and without it on her body, her rash cleared up. When she put it on again, the welts and itchiness returned. She did research and found that reports of similar painful breast conditions had begun surfacing in 2008, all connected to Victoria's Secret bras.

News reports indicated that the culprit seemed to be formaldehyde that apparently appeared in the bras once Victoria's Secret switched from a manufacturer in India to one in China. When Debra told her husband what she had found, he had a quick reaction: *"Burn that bra!"*

Two years after her first blog on bras and allergic reactions, Debra wrote again on the subject under the heading: *"Women still having allergic reactions to Victoria's Secret bras."* She printed letters from her readers including this one:

"My 13-year-old daughter purchased a VS (Victoria's Secret) bra. Three weeks ago with her own money--$40. About that time she started getting welts/hives periodically across her back and chest and up her neck. Couldn't figure it out. Tonight she was getting dressed. Within 2 minutes I watched these long red welts covering her. She's the

one that said, I think it's the bra. She took it off and 20 minutes later they were gone."

Debra commented in response to the letter: *"The really frustrating thing, beyond the fact that this was a 13-year-old girl, is that whatever is causing these allergic reactions (formaldehyde is the leading suspect), Victoria's Secret still isn't slowing down with sales of these harmful products."* The company didn't even put a warning label on the bras *"to alert those who are sensitive to formaldehyde that this product contains trace amounts."*

As for whether consumers have any recourse in this case, Debra answered with: *"People have asked about suing VS, but I think that's a dead end. It's been tried, and it failed. For one thing, their position is that they don't add chemicals to their bras. True enough—the chemicals are already in the fabric and they purchase that fabric after the fact. So, they can legally claim innocence. For another, no one seems to have died from 'contact allergic dermatitis' caused by whatever is in the bra fabric. That said, who knows who might have died from absorbing those chemicals over long periods of time?"*

One of those who did take legal action was Roberta Ritter, who filed a class action lawsuit against Victoria's Secret alleging that the Victoria Secret's bra caused her to have burns, itching, rashes and breast damage. Roberta is an aesthetician and knows her skin and body hence why she felt she had to do something to help other women. She was nauseated, weak and dizzy for two weeks could not work or do anything. Her sister later died of Breast Cancer also wearing the same

Victoria Secrets Bra. Her lawyers did not handle the case properly and it was thrown out of court with no resolve or accountability. She interviewed with us, for the documentary, saying she feels as if it is unresolved, no closure, and she lost her sister without being able to say goodbye. She showed us the burn marks still on her back. When I asked her if she would put the bra back on for us, she went into a post traumatic shock. This book and documentary is for all the women without a voice. Roberta ended the interview saying *"they do not care about us…they only care about themselves and making money."* I know I miss my mother everyday who also passed too early from breast cancer. I would think…out of all the things that scientist and researches for breast cancer would study would be the bra. It would be like researching lung cancer and not looking at the cigarette. We need to direct this further!

Debra De Angelo summarized her feelings and that of her readers this way: *"Those of us who react to the chemicals are the lucky ones—we stop wearing the bras. Those who don't continue to expose themselves to toxins. Who knows how much they have absorbed through the skin, and what those chemicals do once they react a toxic load? Could there be a connection to breast cancer?"* I think you will discover a surprise in the documentary giving Roberta her closure!

An Evolving Connection Emerges

"Breast cancer is the most commonly diagnosed cancer worldwide, and its burden has been rising over the past decades." –The science journal, *Breast*, September 2022.

"We are not anti-bra. We are pro-breast. We believe there are no known health benefits from wearing bras - but there are disturbing parallels between bras and incidents of fibrocystic disease and breast cancer," – Dr. Elizabeth R. Vaughan, American physician.

A connection between chemicals in plastic and breast cancer was first discovered in 1987, at Tufts Medical School in Boston, by research scientists Dr. Ana Soto and Dr. Carlos Sonnenschein. During experiments examining cancer cell growth, plastic test tubes began leaching endocrine-disrupting chemicals, triggering a proliferation of breast cancer cells. They published their findings in the science journal *Environmental Health Perspectives* and it marked a watershed moment in revelations about the relationship between chemicals leaching from plastics and the formation of cancers in humans.

During my interview with Dr. Soto for our documentary in Paris, she described how she and colleagues "had to figure out what else could happen to fetuses exposed to estrogenic chemicals released from plastics. We used bisphenol (BPA), which another group had identified as estrogenic and also present in plastic. We exposed animals to what, to use, seemed to be environmentally relevant doses during pregnancy and then followed their offspring development. The first thing we noticed was that we got much more than we bargained for, namely, we saw some things you'd expect with oestrogens—that is, reproductive effects—but in addition we also noticed obesity and even behavioural problems. It also produced masculinization of the female hypothalamus, alterations in control of ovulation, alterations in development of the mammary gland and increased propensity of the mammary gland to develop cancer." I think the most shocking was Anna informed me that they witnessed fish changing their sex when exposed to these BPAs.

Subsequent research supported her view about the role toxins play in triggering cancer---**85 percent of the 310,720 women in the U.S. diagnosed with breast cancer each year possess no inherited genetic predisposition to this cancer**, meaning the cause is mostly related to lifestyle and environmental factors, including clothing choices that enable the absorption of toxic synthetic chemicals.[33]

We also traveled to a far away farm on the Big island to meet another passionate expert who spent their life studying correlations. Other supporting evidence about bras being connected to cancer emerged from the work of a medical anthropologist, Sydney Ross Singer. Between 1991 and 1993, he and his wife, Soma, conducted a study of 5,000 U.S. women, 30 to 79 years of age, about half with breast cancer, and they discovered the tighter and longer a bra was worn, the higher the incidence of breast cancer, up to 100 times higher,

---

[33] https://www.breastcancer.org/facts-statistics

compared to women who were bra-free. The bra-free women had about the same incidence of breast cancer as men!

This study had been inspired by the time the Singers had spent in the Pacific islands of Fiji, where half of all Fijian women adhered to cultural traditions and refused to wear Western-style bras. **Those bra-less women weren't getting breast cancer, the working women who did wear bras were coming down with cancer.**

Related research emerged in 1991, from a study published in the *European Journal of Cancer*, in which scientists evaluated data on breast cancer risks from more than 15,000 women. One finding stood out: **"Premenopausal women who do not wear bras had half the risk of breast cancer compared with bra users,"** wrote the study authors.[34]

Could the reason bra wearers often get cancer, and bra-less women rarely do, be related to toxins leaching from fabric and getting concentrated in breast tissue as a result of how restrictive bras can be? In the wake of the Singer's findings and observations, science research began to focus on the toxicity of the synthetic chemicals found in bras.

There was another case study published in 2015 in Kenya, done at the Kenyatta National Hospital and the Nairobi Hospital. Their national breast cancer rates have been climbing, as a poorer country industrializing. They discovered that out of the 700 women wearing bras there was a **significant increase in breast cancer compared to**

---

[34] "Breast size, handedness and breast cancer risk." Hsieh CC. Trichopoulos D. *Eur J Cancer*. 1991.

non-bra wearers. 'The researchers concluded: *"Carcinogens released from blocked lymphatics may cause epigenetic changes impacting on cellular downstream signalling that my culminate in cancer."*

We should keep in mind that the human breast is composed of fatty tissue that hold toxins. The nylon and polyester bras are non-permeable, not allowing the breast to breath, and trapping the off-gassing & leaching of the carcinogens from the material and toxic dye of the bra straight into the fatty tissues. The constriction from the bra cuts off the lymphatic drainage thus creating a perfect green house for cancer. All of our tissues drain through the lymphatics, which is essentially the circulatory pathway of the immune system.

However, unlike arteries and veins, these vessels have no internal pressure. As a result, they are easily compressed by external pressure (a bra, for instance) leading to the congestion of the tissues that would otherwise have been drained. Most ladies wear these bras 10-12 hours a day, even working out and sweating in them some unfortunately longer.

In an article titled, "Integrative Medicine: The Prevention and Complementary Treatment of Breast Cancer", Michael B. Schachter, MD, discussed how: *"It is the job of the lymphatic system of the body to help drain toxic substances from tissues and poor lymphatic drainage may play a role in breast cancer formation... Over 85 percent of the lymph fluid flower from the breast drain to the armpit lymph nodes. Most of the rest drains to the nodes along the breast bone. Bras and other external tight clothing can impede flow. The nature of the bra, the tightness, and the length of time worn, will all influence the degree of blockage of lymphatic drainage. Thus, wearing a bra might contribute to the development of breast cancer as a result of cutting off lymphatic drainage, so that toxic chemicals aren't trapped in the breast."*

To test his theory, Singer compared women in Fiji, half of whom wear bras, half of whom go without. Singer found the bra-wearers get breast cancer at the same rate US women do. But, the Fijian women who don't wear bras have almost no incidence of breast cancer. Both groups share the same living environment and diet. Their study (not medically supported) of over 4,700 women gave the following results:

Women who wore their bras 24 hours per day had a **3 out of 4** chance of developing breast cancer (in their study, n=2056 for the cancer group and n=2674 for the standard group).

Women who wore bras more than 12 hour per day but not to bed had a **1 out of 7** risk

Women who wore their bras less than 12 hours per day had a **1 out of 152** risk.

Women, who wore bras rarely or never, had a **1 out of 168** chance of getting breast cancer. The overall difference between 24 hour wearing and not at all was a 125-fold difference. The Medical profession of course claimed it was a faulted study (not approved by them) but when you have risks falling from **3 in 4** to **1 in 133** you must be rather ignorant to say there is no "bra" effect!

Not to study bras as a potential cause of breast cancer strikes me
—and any reasonable person---as simply absurd, It would be like not
looking at cigarettes for lung cancer…but wait they did avoid looking at
them for 30 years! Watch the film 'Thank you for not smoking'

Here is a personal story worth sharing because it illustrates the
depth of wilful neglect and conflicts of interest existing in the breast
cancer field.

I was asked by a cancer fundraising organization, the Susan G.
Komen Foundation in Santa Monica, Calif., to design a bra for one of
their upcoming events. I agreed to do so because my mom, before she
passed from breast cancer, use to do their fundraising walks and raise
money for them in Tennessee. I helped my mom for I believed it gave
her a sense of hope, as she enjoyed talking to the other ladies about
their journey in overcoming this life-threatening disease.

I drove from Malibu down to the Susan G Komen Foundation's
really nice offices and told them about the beautiful hemp bra I
intended to produce for them, using my plant-based dyes. I gave them
the cost to make the bra and in response, they said they weren't
interested in my "overpriced" sustainable bra. They just wanted a
"normal" cheap bra. I was obviously perplexed. You want me to design
a bra made with synthetics containing known carcinogens, for your
breast cancer victims, for a cancer fundraiser? I honestly couldn't
believe what they were telling me. It didn't make any sense!

(Dy buddy who ran the local LA Komen chapter, from Pepperdine, my old Alma Mater, confided in me. I asked him why they turned down my sustainable plant-based bra and he replied, speaking 'off the record' the foundation's main sponsor is Victoria's Secret. This is posted on the Victoria's Secret website: *"For more than 20 years, we have been a leading corporate supporter of the Susan G. Komen MORE THAN PINK WALK and Race for the Cure series of events. Together, we're working to ensure that breakthrough discoveries continue, and that people facing breast cancer receive the care they need to live longer, better lives."*

Full disclosure: I am doing this book and documentary for my mother, Peggy Lynn Garner, and everyone else's mother who has fallen victim to the carcinogens found in their bras. In my opinion, a fast fashion company with a CEO that puts profit before people probably isn't interested in thoroughly testing their bras for carcinogens, by contrast, a non-profit foundation existing to support cancer victims should be pursuing the causes of those cancers, starting with the bras.

Links Between Bras and Breast Cancer

Given that so many bras sold in the U.S. are manufactured in China, it seems only fitting that some of the most revealing research about bras and possible links to breast cancer would come from science researchers in that country. I have done the closing catwalk show at Shanghai Fashion week and ventured with Greenpeace into Xintang, the denim dyeing capital of the world. I have seen firsthand how the

Pearl River flows like tar from the denim dyeing, as the starch from denim sucks all the oxygen out of the water, thus killing all the river life, and the dyes being petroleum based create a tar slick. Light a match, and the whole river would go up, like it did in the Ohio river, back when we dyed our own clothes in the US. The one powerful photo of the Ohio river on fire started the environmental movement in the US in the 1970s!

A 2023 study examining the cancer chemical risk from Chinese-manufactured bras provides us with a case in point. Six Chinese scientists associated with the National Institute for Nutrition and Health and the Chinese Center for Disease Control and Prevention revealed how they had tested a range of brassiere samples manufactured and sold in five areas of China (and exported abroad), to determine their content of heavy metals left over as residues from the manufacturing process. Altogether, **86 bras were tested and six of them contained high levels of nickel and antimony**, levels high enough to trigger a cancer alert if the bras had been properly tested by the manufacturers or a regulatory agency.

Keep in mind that other toxins that possibly appear in the bras weren't tested for, only heavy metals were targeted. It was speculated by the study authors that users of the bras absorbed the highest concentration of metals from bras with a variety of colours, indicating differences in dyeing and other production processes using heavy metals.[35]

Antimony is a metalloid, like arsenic, used as a catalyst in the production of polyester. It has been linked to cancer risks in humans, including breast cancer as a result of absorption of the heavy metal from bras into breast tissue. "Interactions of antimony with biomolecules and its effects on human health."[36]

Nickel is used in textile dye processes. Exposure to nickel, because it's a metalloestrogen (a binder to oestrogen receptors in breast tissue) has been linked to breast cancer in some science studies.[37]

---

[35] "Occurrence and potential release of heavy metals in female underwear manufactured in China: Implication for women's health." Chen H. Et al. Chemosphere. 2023 November.

[36] Lai Z. Et al. *Ecotoxicology and Environmental Safety*. 2022 March.

[37] "The role of cadmium and nickel in oestrogen receptor signalling and breast cancer: metalloestrogens or not?" Aquino NB. Et al. J Environ Sci Health C Environ Carcinog Ecotoxicol Rev. 2012.

Another significant cause of breast cancer is the consumption of PAH (Polycyclic Aromatic Hydrocarbons) found in coal, oil, and gas which is what our synthetic clothes are made out of and dyed with. **Benzo(a)pyrene is the most carcinogenic of the PAHs. When we consume PAHs in food & water our bodies can metabolise & excrete them. But when they metabolise by non ingestion through our skin they produce intermediate products that react to our DNA to form tightly bound complexes or adducts which is the first step in causing cancer.**

Other bra and breast cancer link studies concerned bra tightness and length of time a bra is worn daily.

() By NOT sleeping in a bra, this study found that premenopausal women lower their breast cancer risk by 60% compared to night time bra wearers.[38]

() Bra tightness and length of time the bra was worn received a study examination in 2016, with 304 Brazilian women, and researchers found those **women who wore bras the longest and tightest had more than twice the frequency of breast cancer.**[39]

---

[38] "Risk factors of breast cancer in women in Guangdong and the countermeasures." Zhang AQ. Et al. J South Med Univ. 2009 July.

[39] "Wearing a Tight Bra for Many Hours a Day is Associated with Increased Risk of Breast Cancer." Da Silva Rios S. Et al. *J Oncology Research and Treatments*. 2016 May.

() Finally, a 2015 study review out of China contrasting the results of 12 case-control studies also found an **increased breast cancer risk for women who wore bras during sleep.**[40]

 Endocrine Disrupters Play Havoc with Breasts

It's now well established that endocrine disrupting chemicals interfere with normal breast development at every stage of life, resulting in an increased risk of breast cancer in later years. Science evidence supporting this idea has slowly but steadily been accumulating.

() PFAS chemicals found in stain resistant fabrics have been shown in science studies to impact oestrogens, thyroid hormones, and testosterone levels in humans, all key indicators for the development of cancers. Other studies provided links between bisphenol-A (BPA) and PFAS exposure and breast cancer. A 2023 study by scientists from three U.S. universities affirmed these linkages by examining blood from 10,000 people and showing associations between breast cancer incidence and exposure to the textile chemicals PFAS and BPA.[41]

() Canadian scientists determined that exposure to certain chemicals, such as those used in textile manufacturing, increase the risk of breast cancer after menopause if the woman had prolonged exposure

---

[40] "Brassiere wearing and breast cancer risk: A systematic review and meta-analysis." So WKW. Et al. *World Journal of Meta-Analysis*. 2015 August.

[41] "Exploratory profiles of phenols, parabens, and per- and ply-fluoroalkyl substances among NHANES study participants in association with previous cancer diagnoses." Cathey AL. Et al. *Journal of Exposure Science & Environmental Epidemiology*. 2023 September.

before 36 years of age. The study examined 556 women diagnosed with breast cancer postmenopausal, aged 50 to 75 years. It was found that each **10 years of exposure to nylon fibers doubled the risk of contracting breast cancer** after menopause. The cause was theorized to be either the synthetic fibers or the chemical used to dye fibers or render them fire-resistant.[42]

() The science journal *Environmental Health Perspectives* published a comprehensive study in 2014 that identified 102 synthetic chemicals, many of them involved with textiles, that had been linked to breast cancer. Most of these chemicals are routinely measured in blood and urine of nearly all people tested. Examples listed include aromatic amines from textile dyes, halogenated solvents from dry cleaning and spot removal, and flame retardants used in plastic clothing. Of the 102 chemicals identified in this study, **75 cause mammary tumours** in rodent experiments.[43]

() Another place for scientists to search for a bras and breast link involves studying a byproduct of polyester manufacturing called aromatic amines, chemicals known to be endocrine disrupters. Three studies in particular indicate a connection between aromatic amines and breast cancer:

---

[42] "Postmenopausal breast cancer and occupational exposures." Labreche F. Et al. *Occupational & Environmental* Medicine. 2010.

[43] "New Exposure Biomarkers as Tools for Breast Cancer Epidemiology, Biomonitoring, and Prevention: A Systematic Approach Based on Animal Evidence." Rudel RA. Et al. Environmental Health Perspectives. 2014 May.

184

--Female plastics factory workers exposed to aromatic amines had up to a 10-fold increase in their breast cancer risk.[44]

--Mammalian cells exposed to aromatic amines in lab experiments produced DNA damage that can produce cancer in human breasts.[45]

--Cancer cells taken from human breasts indicate that aromatic amines did do DNA damage within the cells.[46]

What is interesting with this study above is the correlation of the cigarette to lung cancer study in 1996, published in the journal *Science*, that **provided molecular evidence linking components in tobacco smoke** to **lung cancer. B***a***P (Benzo[a]pyrene which is a PAH)** was shown to cause genetic damage in lung cells identical to the damage observed in the **DNA** of most **malignant lung tumours.** It took **30 years to conclusively prove the linkage.** The tobacco industry didn't want it discovered to hurt their sales and their image, in addition to that little issue of liability. Imagine the lawsuits if the fashion industry ever admitted to the cause & correlation of bras to breast cancer? They have a big incentive to squash any studies showing correlations. If you are reading this, then my life's purpose is fulfilled.

[44] "Cancer mortality and occupational exposure to aromatic amines in rubber tire manufacturing in Poland." De Vocht F. Et al. *Cancer Epidemiology*. 2009.

[45] "Section 12.4. DNA Damage and Repair and Their Role in Carcinogenesis." Lodish H. Et al. *Molecular Cell Biology*. 4th edition. 2000.

[46] "Evidence for the presence of mutagenic arylamines in human breast milk and DNA adducts in exfoliated breast ductal epithelial cells." Thompson PA. Et al. *Environmental and Molecular Mutagenesis* 39. 2002.

Victoria Secret Angels remind me of the Marlboro Man created in 1968, giving the image of a hard rugged cowboy smoking. Real cowboys don't smoke, if anything they dip. But I have only owned two farms, been in rodeos, and have owned & rode horses for 39 years… needless to say, this false image of something toxic and unhealthy being used by a cowboy made the Marlboro brand go from 1% of the market to the 4th best-selling brand in America. Sadly but not surprisingly, four of the Marlboro Men died of smoking-related diseases. Similarly tragic, the angels Christine Handy (41), Nicole Weider (38), Jill Goodacre (48) are Victoria Secret models known to have breast cancer. The Victoria Secret Angels helped create a 7 billion-dollar catalog image. In my opinion, profit should never trump human life or suffering.

--Breast cancer cells sensitive to oestrogen have been studied and it was found that some aromatic amines mimic oestrogen and that increase tumour development.[47]

() A general rule with workout clothes is the more you sweat, the more synthetic chemical toxins you potentially absorb through your skin, depending on the type of fabric you wear. Research from the Center for Environmental Health in 2022, tested a range of sports bras and workout shirts and shorts for the presence of bisphenol A (BPA), a known hormone disrupting chemical, commonly added to polyester-based clothing during the manufacturing process to provide anti-static and colourfast properties.Testing found BPA above safe levels (as

[47] "Mechanisms of action of the carcinogenic heterocyclic amine PhIP." Gooderham N. Et al. *Toxicology Letters*. 2007.

mandated under California's Proposition 65 law) in polyester-based sports bras by such firms as *Amazon Essentials, Avia, Just Be, Patagonia and Skechers*. [48]

() Indication of that class of chemicals called PFAS, added to clothing as a water and stain resistant finish, were reported to be detected in women's sports bras during lab testing commissioned by the safety blog, Mamavation, during 2022. Mamavation reported that **23 sports bras tested yielded chemical indicators of PFAS,** ranging from 58 ppm (parts per million) in Third Love Muse Sports bras, 57 ppm in Adidas Don't Rest Alphaskin Bra, 48 ppm in Champion Freedom Seamless Racerback Sports Bra, 48 ppm in SheFit Sports Bra, to 38 ppm in Nike Women's Medium Support Non-Padded Sports Bra. Other name brands included in the testing survey were UnderArmour, Lane Bryant, Old Navy.[49]

Finding PFAS chemicals in sports bras should concern any physically active female because these 'forever' chemicals persist within human bodies for years. Certain PFAS's are known endocrine disrupters that alter human metabolism, fertility, reduce fetal growth, advance the risk of becoming overweight or obese, and most dangerously, to increase your risk of cancers, including breast cancer. [50]

---

[48] "New Testing Shows High Levels of BPA in Sports Bras and Athletic Shirts." The Center for Environmental Health. October 12, 2022.

[49] "In Depth: First-of-its kind testing points to dangers and unknowns of PFAS in clothing." Elizabeth Gribkoff. *Environmental Health News*. Feb. 15, 2022. https://www.ehn.org/pfas-clothing-2656587709.html

[50] "Per-and Polyfluoroalkyl Substance Toxicity and Human Health Review: Current State of Knowledge." Fenton SE. Et al. *Environ Toxicol Chem*. 2012 March.

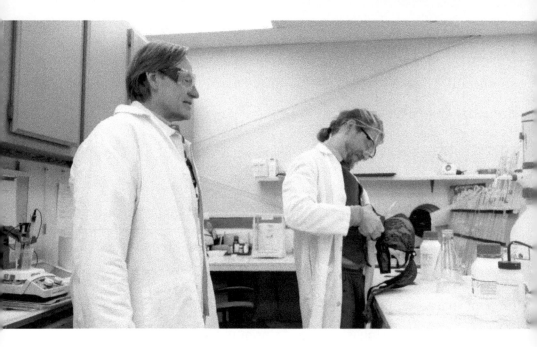

Darin Olien & Jeff at the lab testing the bra

Having toxicologists do lab testing of every individual chemical for its cancer potential may end up costing the health and life of countless people because the process is slow and expensive. Testing for entire classes of toxic substances, such as PFASs, containing dozens or hundreds of chemicals, would be more health protective, effective, and less expensive, as we argue in Chapters 7 and 8.

Artist Wonderment

A Common Sense Regulatory Solution

"As communities around the country grapple with PFAS contamination, this adds further evidence that supports policymakers developing action to reduce PFAS exposure. Since PFAS make up thousands of chemicals, one way to reduce exposures is for EPA (U.S. Environmental Protection Agency) to regulate PFAS as a class of chemicals, rather than one at a time." --- Dr. Tracey J. Woodruff, co-author of a study linking PFAS to breast and other cancers.

Chemicals That Shake the Bedrock of Humankind

The Earth's environment and living species including man are being increasingly affected by the growing numbers and quantities of chemical compounds produced by various industry. Despite warnings given in the early sixties, the proliferation of polluting agents has continued unabated. One effect has been the alarming rise in obesity, male infertility, cancer and cardiovascular diseases. The term endocrine disrupter was adopted at the Wingspread Conference to define biologically harmful industrial products. That factor is now a major health hazard on a global scale. It is urgently necessary to screen all chemicals for endocrine disrupting effects before allowing their use or release into the environment. ---Scientists Dr. Ana Soto and Dr. Carlos Sonnenschein, Professors at Tufts University School of Medicine, in *World Affairs*, Summer 2007.

Naked

Chapter VI: Nature Can't Heal Itself Alone

Another Planetary Boundary Has Been Breached

"While chemicals provide many desired benefits, they may be released during their lifecycle, and cause adverse effects on human health and the environment. Indeed, chemical pollution has now been recognized as one of the 'planetary boundaries' (the planetary environmental limits within which humanity can safely operate), and it adversely impacts other planetary boundaries such as climate change and biosphere integrity." --"Toward a Global Understanding of Chemical Pollution: A First Comprehensive Analysis of National and Regional Chemical Inventories." Wang Z. Et al. *Environmental Science & Technology.* 2020 January.

 A 'Laundry List' of Pollution Violations

"The fashion industry is one of the largest polluters in the world. Water pollution, release of toxic chemicals, textile waste, greenhouse gas emissions, soil pollution, and rainforest degradation are some of the environmental impacts of this industry." *–Plastic Soup Foundation, Amsterdam, 2022.*

Billy Gibbons (ZZ Top), Phil Collen (Def Leppard), & Jimmy Choo

When I began to design in Nashville, Tennessee, for my band buddies from Lynard Skynard, Def Leppard, Taylor Swift, Amy Grant, Barry Manilow etc, I realized very quickly how dirty the garment industry could be. I started out designing band t-shirts using adobe illustrator to draw my designs on the very first green Mac Pro Computer. At the time and still today screen printing utilizes a very toxic plastisol ink that contains PFAS, along with heavy metals, formaldehyde, etc. One of the reasons children are found to have PFAS in their blood due to all the printed garments they are wearing right under their nose.

Seeing the workers wearing masks while pulling newly printed t-shirts off a dryer made me realize that either I had to quit doing what I love, or figure out a different solution. I remember clearly how everyone working in the screen-printing facility had acne on their faces…and none of them were teenagers…I could hardly breathe and I asked them to open up their garage doors because when PVC inks are heated for drying, they off gas toxic fumes called Dioxins and Furans. The dye houses were not any prettier or cleaner.

Washing/Drying Leaches Out Microfibers

Science studies from our friends at 5 Gyres Institute document how the laundering of plastic-based synthetic fabrics and clothing using washing machines causes the shedding of dense blizzards of tiny plastic fibers. These microplastics are too small to be caught by conventional filtration systems within washing machines, nor are they filtered out by municipal water treatment plants. Instead, these fibers flow out into the environment as contaminants via wastewater effluent. We interviewed Madder industries owner, Adam Root, based in Bristol, UK for the doc whose research found that the number one source of plastics in the ocean is from Textiles![1]

To be considered a microfiber it needs to be less than 5 mm in size and threadlike in shape. The vast majority shed from synthetic fleece and polyester garments. Considering that normal garment care results in many dozens of washing cycles for each individual garment annually, added to the estimated 100 billion new pieces of clothing manufactured globally each year, you might begin to sense how gigantic the problem of environmental contamination by microfibers is becoming.[2]

---

[1] "Microfibers, Macro problems." The 5 Gyres Institute. November 2017.

[2] "Microfibers, Maco problems: A resource guide and toolkit for understanding and tackling the problem of plastic microfiber pollution in our communities." Roisin Magee Altreuter. The 5 Gyres Institute. 2017 November

Scientists in 2021 evaluated the laundry release from a variety of synthetic and natural textile samples during five consecutive laundry washing cycles and found that microfiber loss for each garment ranged from 9.6 mg to 1,240 mg per wash. **Polyester clothing samples released six times more microfibers than did nylon and other fiber types.**[3]

Madder Industries has created a solution filter to capture these smaller particles and during his interview he summed up the antagonism we are up against *"The Triangle.. big business billion dollars going this way and a million pounds building a kids playground…you got the academics that are being paid to research the problem but not to solve it…if you can continue to fund the program you can continue to research things but your not about solutions and then you got the crazy hippies which is us causing noise but we found the big corporations will fund groups to discredit the movement and stop the change at a global scale. Academics publishing papers of findings not in the interest of big business and getting sued to remove these findings. If you create linkage they will sue for then legislation will have to act for it is a public health issue. Like bras to breast cancer."* Adam Root

Having loose ends (fuzz) on a garment produces more microfiber shedding during a wash, a process that also accelerates with

---

[3] "Domestic laundry and microfiber pollution: Exploring fiber shedding from consumer apparel textiles." Vassilenko E. Et al. *PLoS One*. 2021 July.

higher water temperatures and the more rotations per minute each clothing item undergoes in a washing machine.[4]

Once the washing cycle is finished, detergents remaining in the wastewater either get discharged directly into the environment, or get partially removed in a treatment plant. Huge amounts of detergents still end up in the environment because of the volume of laundry wastewater that must be treated, and that places aquatic and terrestrial ecosystems at risk as a result of the endocrine disrupters in detergents, affecting the reproductive systems of fish.[5]

Not even the household dryers used to complete the washing process are without a role to play in generating fibers. As researchers reported in a 2022 science journal study: *"A single tumble dryer could be responsible for releasing 120 million synthetic microfibers into the air each year and are one of the main sources of microfiber pollution in the atmosphere."*[6]

To enhance the antibacterial and anti-odor properties of garments, especially socks and underwear, some manufacturers have added silver nanoparticles to fabrics. Research shows that nanosilver leaches out of the fabrics during washing and this nanosilver can be

---

[4] "Microfibers generated from the laundering of cotton, rayon and polyester based fabrics and their aquatic biodegradation." Zambrano MC. Et al. *Marine Pollution Bulletin*, 2019.

[5] "Surfactants in aquatic and terrestrial environment: occurrence, behaviour, and treatment processes." Jardak K. Et al. *Environ Sci Pollut Res*. 2016.

[6] "Microfibers Released into the Air from a Household Tumble Dryer." Tao D. Et al. *Environmental Science & Technology*. 2022.

Outside Jakarta, Indonesia we discovered the burning of access garments on the beach

toxic to both humans and aquatic life. (It can harm human liver cells, skin and lungs.)

Observed Sukalyan Sengupta, a professor of wastewater treatment at the University of Massachusetts: "Once silver goes down the drain and ends up at wastewater treatment plants, it can potentially harm bacterial treatment processes, making them less efficient, and foul treatment equipment. More than 90% of silver nanoparticles released in wastewater end up in nutrient-rich biosolids left over at the end of sewage treatment, which often are used on land as agricultural fertilizers. This poses multiple risks. If plants take up silver from soil, they could concentrate it and introduce it into the food chain."[7]

---

[7] "Silver nanoparticles in clothing wash out—and may threaten human health and the environment." Sukalyan Sengupta and Tabish Nawaz. The Conversation. March 202, 2018.

Chemical allergens benzothiazole, benzotriazole, and quinoline and their derivatives are widely used in garment manufacturing as stabilizers in the dye process. Scientists analyzed 27 clothing samples before, and after five and then ten times of washing cycles. Benzothiazole was detected in 85% of the clothing samples, followed by quinoline found in 81% of samples. The researchers reported: "The average decrease in concentration for benzothiazoles was 50% after ten washing cycles and around 20% for quinolines…these results strongly indicate that laundering of clothing textiles can be an important source of release of these compounds to household wastewater and in the end, to aquatic environments. **It also demonstrates a potential source of human exposure to these {potentially harmful} chemicals since considerable amounts of the compounds remain in the clothes even after ten times of washing."**[8]

Three scientists on the Faculty of Science and Engineering, at Maastricht University in The Netherlands, analyzed the world's polyester clothing value chain in 2021, and concluded that upwards of **one-fifth of all global water pollution** has can be traced to the wastewater carrying **chemicals used in dyeing and finishing textiles.** Laundry effluent alone may account for 35% of global microplastic pollution in oceans.[9]

---

[8] "The washout effect during laundry on benzothiazole, benzotriazole, quinoline, and their derivatives in clothing textiles." Luongo G. Et al. *Environ Sci Pollut Res Int*. 2016 February.

[9] "Analysis of the polyester clothing value chain to identify key intervention points for sustainability." Palacios-Mateo C. Et al. *Environ Sci Eur*. 2021. "Primary microplastics in the oceans: a global evaluation of sources." IUCN . 2017.

Fabric Disposal Methods Multiply Harm

"Effluents and sludge from {fabric} production processes cannot be safely deposited into ecosystems, so they are often buried or burned as hazardous waste. The fabric itself is sold all over the world, used, then thrown away—which usually means it is either incinerated, releasing toxins, or placed in a landfill. Even in the rather short life span of the fabric, its particles have abraded into the air and been taken into people's lungs." -- Cradle to Cradle: Remaking the Way We Make Things, by Michael Braungart and William McDonough, 2002.

New Disposal Innovations Awaited

We discovered on the distant beaches in Indonesia, about an eight-hour journey from Jakarta, a desolate fishing village where remnants of half-burned clothing covered the entire beach. It was shocking and smelled horrible. My team could barely stay there, even as we saw fishermen going out to fish for their supper. I walked in the blackened water with an open sore on my foot thinking about the disease I might receive from documenting this powerful visual to show the world.

We consume too much. Fast Fashion will eat itself from the inside out…it is a selfish, wasteful, and horrible model that must end. As for burning toxic chemical clothing the conventional way, which some recommend, you might as well drop an atomic bomb given the amount of carcinogenic chemicals that go airborne and into the sea and sand. This is not the answer.

One time I met with a NASA scientist working on a new type of incinerator that he wanted to place on a boat and take it out to sea to the 5 gyres floating plastic dump. He said he could incinerate the trash and take it back to its natural form, whether gas or liquid, to use for energy. Now that's a solution worth investing in!

 . **Unmanaged and Unregulated**

Recent studies from across the globe suggest that microfibers are in fact the most common type of plastic polluting our oceans today. The flow of microfibers into our oceans is not currently being managed or regulated, making these invisible and ubiquitous plastics a major environmental and human health concern that requires action in our communities now. [10]

---

[10] "Microfibers, Maco problems: A resource guide and toolkit for understanding and tackling the problem of plastic microfiber pollution in our communities." Roisin Magee Altreuter. The 5 Gyres Institute. 2017 November.

Chain Reactions Occurring Throughout the Environment

"Chemical clothing affects the health of the entire planet, from the toxic production methods used, to the chemicals employed in the cleaning of these items, to clothing disposal practices that allow these non-biodegradable products to continue to harm the environment long after their users have ceased to exist." –*Killer Clothes: How Seemingly Innocent Clothing Choice Endanger Your Health*, by Anna Maria and Brian Clement, 2011.

Redesign the Entire Textile Chain

Recognising that textile production is the world's second most polluting industry, second to the oil industry, a team of five textile engineers and scientists from Australia, Pakistan and China, issued this challenge in 2021: Textiles are essential to humans in a variety of ways, especially clothing. However, the speed at which they end up in landfills is astonishing **(one garbage truck per second)**, posing a severe risk to the environment, if the trend continues. Governments and responsible organizations are starting to make calls to different stakeholders to redesign the textile chain from linear to circular economy. In this perspective, we highlight some of the possible approaches to be undertaken including the need for the creation of renewable raw materials sources, rethinking production, maximum use and reuse of textile productions, reproduction, and recycling strategies, redistribution of textiles to new and parallel markets, and improvising means to extend the textiles lifetime.[11]

Among the points made:

() About **73% of fibers used in clothing "ends up either in landfill or an incinerator with only 12% recycled**…new fibers can be readily blended with old recycled fibers to strike the right balance between quality and sustainability."[2]

() "It is estimated that around **98% of all future fibers will be synthetic, 95% of which is expected to be polyester**. The rise in synthetics poses an environmental concern due to many reasons in various perspectives. The production of synthetic polymers is estimated to utilize **98 million tons of oil** globally each year which can be used directly as fibers, dyes, and finishes, hence dependent on fossil fuel extraction. Synthetic fibers are non-biodegradable. They can stay in the environment for many years."

⚜ Fibers Surround Us and Penetrate Us

() **Microfibers released into the air and water have spread everywhere on the planet, even into the Arctic.** Not surprisingly, given their ubiquitous presence in the environment, microfibers entered

[11] "Circular Economy and Sustainability of the Clothing and Textile Industry." Chen X. Et al. Materials Circular Economy. 2021 July.

the food chain and have been detected in many organisms, as well as in fruit and vegetable crops.[12]

() **Drinking water supplies are infiltrated**. Noted a 2017 science paper: "Microfibers have been isolated from tap water in a study that tested more than 150 samples from all over the world."[13]

() **Polyester fibers have been found in the snow on Mount Everest**, much of it near camp sites, shed from the clothing of climbers.[14]

() **Microfibers have been detected in deep sea sediments** and in mussels from the Dutch and Belgian coasts.[15]

() **Aquatic life consumes microfiber plastics**. Much microfiber pollution ends up in the oceans and lakes as runoff or as residues of wastewater treatment plants. Because microfibers are similar in size to plankton, many species of aquatic life, from fish to whales and shellfish, consume them and in turn, when humans eat this aquatic life, these fibers are ingested and end up in the bodies of humans.[16]

() **Is any aquatic life immune to disruption?** As of 2020, **microfibers showed up in 20% of Icelandic cod, 17 % of red mullet**

[12] "Microplastic in marine organism, environmental and toxicological effects." Guzzetti E. Et al. *Environ Toxicol Pharmacol*. 2018. And "Micro- and nano-plastics in edible fruit and vegetables. The first diet risks assessment for the general population." Conti G. Et al. *Environm Res. 2020.*

[13] "Synthetic polymer contamination of global drinking water." Kosuth M. Et al. *PLoS ONE*. 2017.

[14] "Reaching new heights in plastic pollution—preliminary findings of microplastics on Mount Everest." Napper IE. Et al. One Earth. 2020.

[15] "Microplastics en route: Field measurements in the Dutch river delta and Amsterdam canals, wastewater treatment plants, North Sea sediments and biota. Leslie HA. Et al. *Environ Int*. 2017.

[16] "Microfibers, Macro problems." The 5 Gyres Institute. November 2017.

from the Mediterranean **and 15% of sardines** off the coast of Spain. Fibers have been measured in plankton, seagulls, turtles, seals and fish. Absorption of fibers can cause inflammatory responses, metabolic disturbances, cellular damage, and toxicity to specific organs.[17]

() **As microplastic pollution increases, insect populations dwindle**. As an illustration, over the past decade a 60% reduction in insect populations has been observed in German forests. Insects easily absorb micro and microplastics in their bodies and pass it up the food chain as they are eaten. Bees have been documented bringing microplastics into hives where the fibers end up in the honey and larvae.[18]

 ## Inconvenient Truths About Clothing Microfibers

Since we are constantly shedding microfibers/microplastics from our clothing during ordinary wear and from the washing and drying of clothes, we cannot separate ourselves and our actions from the greater environment. These fibers are having measurable and harmful health impacts on our bodies in some ways that mirror impacts on the surrounding environment.

"Throughout a lifetime of exposure to microplastic via different food types and inhalation, children and adults are estimated to take in

---

[17] "Microplastic ingestion by fish: Body size, condition factor and gut fullness are not related to the amount of plastics consumed." De Vries AN. Et al. *Marine Pollution Bulletin*. 2020.

[18] "Is There a Connection Between Dramatic Insect Deaths and Microplastics?" Plastic Soup Foundation. April 21, 2023.

553 particles/capita/day {children} and 883 particles/capita/day {adults} respectively, measured in the gut, body tissue, and stool." [19]

"In major world cities such as **Paris and London, the outdoor air contains large amounts of fibers, of which 29% {Paris}and 17% {London} respectively consisted of purely petrochemical-based plastic (e.g. synthetic) fibers.** The air we breathe is polluted with microplastics."[20]

"Once {microplastics} have been inhaled or ingested, they can migrate to various organs in humans and animals, such as liver, kidneys, brain and placenta…the full extent of that exposure and the consequences are still relatively poorly understood."[21]

An Asian study done in 2022 found that about **one-third of the dust measured** in air conditioning filters from living rooms, offices and dormitories were **microplastic fibers of polyester and rayon**.[22]

"Children under the age of 6 inhale 3 times more microplastics than an average adult. This was concluded in a study of Sydney {Australia} homes which showed that Australian estimates of deposition and inhalation rates are at the lower end of the exposure spectrum compared to other similar studies in other parts of the world. Young

---

[19] "Lifetime Accumulation of Microplastic in Children and Adults. Mohamed Nor NH. Et al. *Environmental Science & Technology*. 2021.

[20] "Do Clothes Make Us Sick? Fashion, Fibers and Human Health." Plastic Soup Foundation, 2022. www.plasticsoupfoundation.org

[21] "Microplastics in air: Are we breathing it in?" Gasperi J. Et al. *Current Opinion in Environmental Science and Health*. 2018.

[22] "Air conditioner filters become sinks and sources of indoor microplastics fibers." Chen Y. Et al. *Environmental Pollution*. 2022.

children {under five years of age} inhale twice the amounts of synthetic fibers and ingest twelve times more than adults over 20 years of age because small children have greater natural hand-to-mouth activities as part of their normal developmental behaviours. Furthermore, young children spend much time crawling around on the floor and thus have a higher exposure risk to microplastic particles, including synthetic fibers. Children are most likely to be at risk from adverse effects because their systems are developing."[23]

Some scientists predict that microfiber accumulation, at all layers of life, could ultimately threaten world food security and biodiversity.

 Microfiber Impacts: Wide-Ranging and Multiplying

() **An industry with a large carbon footprint**. As the European Union statistical agency Eurostat has observed: "The transport {between countries or regions} of raw materials, fibers/yarns, fabrics and garments, and all the chemicals needed at each stage, adds up to a large carbon footprint that contributes to global warming."[24]

() **Each production step of the fashion industry negatively impacts the environment** with its water, material, chemical and energy use. More than half of all garments are now made of oil-derived polyester and water usage alone amounts to 79 trillion litres of water

[23] "Quantification and exposure assessment of microplastics in Australian indoor house dust." Soltani NS. Et al. *Environmental Pollution,* 2021.

[24] "How are emissions of greenhouse gases by the EU evolving?" Eurostat, 2020.

per year. A disturbing 8-10% of all global CO2 emissions are attributable to the fashion industry.[25]

() **Microplastics even alter weather patterns**. Researchers writing in the American Chemical Society's journal, *Environmental Science & Technology Letters*, reported that microplastics had been detected in a majority of cloud samples taken in 2023 from a Chinese mountaintop. Computer modeling indicated these tiny microplastics had been lofted into wind currents from nearby highly populated Chinese cities. Like dust particles, these microplastic particles attract water droplets to form around them, resulting in cloud formation.[26]

Japanese scientists also reported in 2023 how they had climbed Mount Fuji and Mount Oyama and collected water samples from clouds. They i**dentified nine different types of polymers in the clouds, finding up to 14 microplastic particles in each liter of cloud water collected**, demonstrating that 'plastic air pollution' is a real and growing problem. "When microplastics reach the upper atmosphere and are exposed to ultraviolet radiation from sunlight, they break down and contribute to greenhouse gases," warned study co-author Hiroshi Okochi of Waseda University.[27]

---

[25] "The environmental price of fast fashion." Niinimaki K. Et al. *Nature Reviews Earth & Environment*. 2020.

[26] "Characterization of Microplastics in Clouds over Eastern China." Xu X. Et al. Environ Sci Technol Lett. 2023 November.

[27] "Airborne hydrophilic microplastics in cloud water at high altitudes and their role in cloud formation." Wang Y. Et al. *Environmental Chemistry Letters*. 2023 August.

ᵀoxic Environments Within *And* Outside of Us

As within, as without…our inner world mirrors the outer one in ways other than just metaphorical. Toxins are in our crops, our fish, and in our bellies. They penetrate our skin every day and flow through us, migrating from the clothing we wear, just as they migrate into the .natural world every day riding on currents of water and air.

Flight attendants typically wear synthetically dyed toxic polyester PFAS coated uniforms mandated by the companies they work for. American Airlines, United, Alaska, and Delta airlines all had lawsuits regarding their uniforms. The uniforms were stated that they do not breathe, cause rashes, burns, and breathing issues not mention future health implications. To their credit, the airline employees protested and attempted go through our legal system to stop the contamination.

Monica, the flight attendant that filed the original lawsuit, who we interviewed for the doc was not wrong that there was something bad going on to her and her friend's bodies from this uniform. They just did not know what to test for. As a designer, in my opinion, we are responsible for what we use to make something (ingredients), how it is made (manufacturing), and how it affects the person wearing it (health application). Then it boils down to consciousness and ethics when it comes to those choices.

Often, I talk about how I believe in free markets and commerce, but not at the price of human life. Why should that statement even be considered controversial? I would rather live in the woods naked with my family safe from toxins, living off the land, than taking part in an industry knowingly using toxic chemicals in their products while denying they cause any harm. I would also do anything to bring back my daughter who died from crop dusting chemicals and my mother who died of breast cancer which I believe was caused by the nylon polyester bras.

Ꞃaving the clothing industry set the ppm (parts per million) levels of what toxins it deems safe is like asking a Hippo to self-regulate its appetite in front of a fridge full of Sunday roast. Equally absurd is that consumers too often expect large corporations to do 'the right thing' and not only comply with government regulations, but go 'beyond the call of duty' when these regulations or non-existent or don't go far enough in the face of obvious threats to health.

Similar to the Volkswagen Scandal when they deliberately circumvented U.S. EPA emissions laws on the so-called clean diesel models sold from 2009-2015. Volkswagen admitted that it equipped the control software for its 2.0-liter TDI diesel vehicles with a "defeat device" that detected when the car was undergoing emissions testing and significantly changed the operations of its powertrain to reduce emissions during the tests. Best part of the story is that it wasn't discovered by the EPA at all, but by a clean-air group that tested VW diesel models to confirm its hypothesis that the latest diesel cars complied with all emissions standards while remaining much more efficient than comparable gasoline cars. The U.S. Environmental Protection Agency doesn't test every new car for emissions compliance every year. Instead, manufacturers **"self-certify"** and submit their data to the EPA....sound familiar?

There are plenty of examples of smaller individuals and companies doing the right thing by choosing safety over profits… and thousands of examples of cowards keeping the masses addicted to products they know to be harmful. How can these compromised owners and corporate executives sleep peacefully at night?

I decided to commit my life to making a difference… for the sake of our internal environment…for the sake of our external environment…no matter what the cost might be to my reputation and my own comfort zone.

Madeira Lace Portugal Collection shot in Madeira Island

⚜ On the Cutting Edge of Denial

"We deny because we have become addicted to the conveniences of modern life, just as the ancient Romans became complacent about their lifestyle addictions that proved toxic to their health. We deny because our arrogance blinds us to the lessons of history. We deny because we choose to believe that we are too wise to be so foolish." *—The Hundred-Year Lie*, Randall Fitzgerald, 2006.

Chapter VII: Solutions: Can We See the Light?

Being Denied a Fundamental Consumer Right

"Lowering safety and production standards and product quality to increase bottom-line profits, while knowingly and deceptively selling consumers inferior, defective, or unhealthy products, has long been a standard business strategy. Every day, substandard, defective, toxic, even dangerous products are knowingly released into the market and sold to the public. At the same time and in the same way, we are also being denied a fundamental consumer right—the right to know exactly what we are being sold and are consuming, and what the effects of the things we are sold and consume can have on our bodies, our health, and on the environment." –Horst M. Rechelbacher, cosmetics corporate CEO, author of *Minding Your Business: Profits That Restore the Planet*, 2008.

Covering Up the Identities of Chemicals

"Over **350,000 chemicals** and mixtures of chemicals **have been registered for production and use** {worldwide} up to three times as many as previously estimated and with substantial differences across countries/regions. A noteworthy finding is that the identities of many chemicals remain publicly unknown because they are claimed as confidential (over 50,000) or ambiguously described (up to 70,000). Coordinated efforts by all stakeholders including scientists from different disciplines are urgently needed." [1]

Big Red

---

[1] –"Toward a Global Understanding of Chemical Pollution: A First Comprehensive Analysis of National and Regional Chemical Inventories." Wang Z. Et al. Environmental Science & Technology. 2020.

⚜ Payback for Doing the 'Right Thing'

ⒹMy first arrest occurred at the age of 10, near my family farm in Tennessee. I drove my Big Red 3 -Wheeler to the next-door park where they were about to bulldoze some of my favorite ancient Oak trees. I cut the wires of those bulldozers to stop this awful sinful act…why would anyone kill beautiful 200 year old Oak trees to make a park?

Soon after my last cut I heard the sirens and so I did what any country boy raised on *Dukes of Hazard* would do and jumped back on my 250 CC 3 -Wheeler and drove in high gear. I raced through the woods and sure enough lost him, until I decided to go back and help him push the cop car out of the mud!

ⒹMy mamma raised me right…I was doing the right thing both in cutting those wires and helping the cop in trouble. Too bad he did not see it that way. I ended up going on probation that year and my dad was devastated. Devil child!

Mother

What We Don't Know Is Hurting Us

(Manufacturers and regulatory agencies try to reassure us that the small levels of toxins in each piece of synthetic clothing can't and won't harm our health, either in the short or the long term. But they honestly do not know, therefore, we should not feel reassured. I was around designing and producing before all the textile certification programs emerged…and we should be specific, it's 'textile' not 'dyes' and not 'garment', just the textile that's the focus of certification.

Think about all the additives inserted after the fabric is made. Imagine all the dye stuffs full of toxins. As a result, do these certification programs actually help the consumer? No, not really…do they make money…yes…and maybe they help sell a product. But don't fall for the marketing idea that the garment is pure and free from chemicals that could hurt you. That just isn't a certifiable fact.

If a manufacturer is doing something right, with good intentions, then why would it need to be certified? Until they start having independent labs testing the final product of every production run then the certification programs cannot be trusted by the consumer. It is just marketing and business to seem as if it is regulating.

I started a kids collection called 'Sustainable Kids' back when my first daughter was born. I did 10 styles and sold it to Nordstroms. I had no idea what I was doing but I was doing it and with good intentions. Though I could never compete with the mainstream guys, I am proud to say I was the first designer to bring Nordstroms a product that was truly sustainable. We had a give back program with a printed box at the point of purchase (register) with needs for my buddy's orphanage in Haiti and we paid for the postage. The idea was when you buy something new you give something old away as a teaching lesson for your child. Nordstroms loved it!

Then one day I was leaving for London Fashion Week to show my latest couture collection and my production manager called me and says the company returned the baby onesie because the sleeve ribbing was a slightly different off white than the body. Guess who could not eat for the year? So there went the first sustainable kid's line at Nordstroms, but I had the best intentions. Red Light!

Over 80,000 chemicals are sold in the US (out of more than 300,000 worldwide) and the Environmental Protection Agency *has **only banned nine*** as dangerous to health. The EPA has had the power to regulate harmful chemicals under the Toxic Substances Control Act since 1976, but the EPA relies on chemical companies to be responsible and ethical to report the chemicals they are using, along with studies to show if these chemicals are harmful to the environment. **Human health** isn't discussed as criteria for EPA compliance.

Imagine being an executive with a multi-million-dollar fashion company and the organization that's supposed to test and regulate your product says to you, do your own testing and just send us the paperwork, but only if we ask you to!

Perhaps this very ethical CEO, who has to answer to his board and ultimately, to shareholders in the company, would do the right thing. If he or she found too many toxins in their polyester nylon puff jacket that's their number one seller, these executives would do the right thing and willingly sacrifice a big share of their profits and immediately take the product off the market to protect public health. How often does that happen? I think we all know the answer. However, in our documentary journey we did discover one company, Icebreaker, that did make this sacrifice and took their number 1 item off the sales table until they could make it out of wool and sure enough after 5 years that made their money back and are no longer producing that deathly jacket. This gives me hope!

Over the decades I have not discovered one company in the fashion industry that does toxin testing on their finished garment…not one! They will instead declare how this product is certified (independently tested) and contains only so many PPM (parts per million) of this carcinogenic chemical, making it below the legal limit (by the way the apparel industry sets the legal limit). As for the certifications, you can pay for them and publicize only the results you want, and if you dig deeper, you find that to be certified just applies to the raw fabric or yarn, not the final garment after it has been dyed and finished. It is like my buddy's dog who just peed on the restaurant couch is also a "certified" service dog…lol.

So who really regulates, who really exercises oversight? In the U.S. the Chemical Data Reporting (CDR) rule, under the Toxic

Substances Control Act (TSCA), requires manufacturers (including importers) to provide EPA with information on the production and use of chemicals in commerce. The Toxic Substances Control Act (TSCA) of 1976 provides EPA with authority to require reporting, record-keeping and testing requirements, and restrictions relating to chemical substances and/or mixtures.

Ꮋow is that working? Take the example of disperse blue I dye, which has caused malignant urinary, bladder, and lung tumours in lab animal studies. Not even manufacturers of this dye can reasonably dispute the science findings. Yet, this is what the National Toxicology Program of the U.S. Department of Health and Human Services has to say about Disperse blue I dye used on polyester, nylon, cellulose acetate, acrylate fibers, and on fur and sheepskin:

"Ꮯhe last reported quantity for U.S. production of disperse blue I {a *reasonably anticipated to be a human carcinogen*} was over 350,500 lb in 1972 (IARC 1990); after 1972, *production figures specifically for disperse blue I were no longer reported.* Production in the United States, by one company, was last reported in 1992 (HSDB 2009). **In 2009, no commercial manufacturers of disperse blue I were identified worldwide (SRI 2009), but *disperse blue I was available from five suppliers,*** *including three U.S. suppliers* (ChemSources 2009). *No data on U.S. imports or exports of disperse blue I were found.*"[2]

---

[2] "Report on Carcinogens, Fifteenth Edition." National Toxicology Program. U.S. Department of Health and Human Services.

Let's digest these revelations for a moment. It's important to recognize and underscore what this U.S. government monitoring and regulatory agency admits publicly (if you can find it): *the agency doesn't know whether a carcinogenic chemical used on clothing is being imported or exported by U.S. manufacturers, or even whether this cancer agent is being sold in the U.S.* This admission exposes how consumers face documented health hazards that remain mostly unidentified.

Consider another piece of evidence exposing the gap in consumer protection systems. Allergy Standards, a non-governmental company based in Ireland, describes itself as 'a clean green' product certification service that operates worldwide, certifying the safety of consumer products that include textiles and clothing. (www.allergystandards.com) Among the textile chemicals this certifier pays close attention to its monitoring of formaldehyde (a cause of contact dermatitis, skin irritation, and respiratory problems), Azo dyes composing 80% of all colorants (causing contact dermatitis and possibly cancer), Organotin compounds used as an anti-odor additive (it affects the human immune and reproductive systems), and Chlorobenzenes used in dyeing for polyester (toxic by skin contact).

This certification service identifies a serious problem with those five chemicals, signalling the problems in general with the monitoring process of toxins in clothing: **"Manufacturers can source textiles from anywhere in the world, which has many benefits, but also raises many questions. For example, how does a clothing**

manufacturer in Los Angeles know that a textile producer in India, China or Europe is producing clothing that complies with the chemical limits {of various countries or the European Union}. The State of California has the lowest limit levels in the U.S., on par with the EU. However, where long supply chains are concerned, how can manufacturers know for certain if limit levels were adhered to?"[3]

With so many thousands of chemicals to keep and lose track of, and so few resources devoted to regulatory agencies testing for the presence of toxic chemicals in clothing, chemical safety is mostly left to each company operating at every stage of the supply chain to pass on the identities of chemicals added to the production process. This is an inherently flawed system was erected to insure production efficiency and bottom-line profits, rather than to protect public safety and health.

⚜ Too Many Regulations That Don't Make Sense

"There's a problem with the way the United States and other countries look at toxicity in commercial agents. Regulators nowadays often won't take action until enough people have already complained of harm. This makes little sense. People have a right to know whether products they use on themselves and their children contain compounds that increase their risk of disease."[4]

---

[3] "What chemicals are in Textiles and the Health Implications." Allergy Standards. www.allergystandards.com/news_events/chemicals-in-textiles-and-the-health-implications/

[4] –Dr. Devra Davis, professor of epidemiology, in *Newsweek*, 2007

𝔊oo Few Regulations Adequately Enforced

It must be **proven by scientific study that a chemical causes either cancer… or death… before it is required to be taken off the market** in the U.S. Meanwhile, the manufacturers can focus on minimizing their costs without serious oversight.

𝔊his U.S. Toxic Substances Control Act of 1976 allows chemicals to be sold and used by consumers unless these chemicals are proven to be a risk to health. Yet, the EPA doesn't do the safety testing, it relies on manufacturers to conduct its own tests for compliance. **The fox designs the chicken coop…**how brilliant is that!

In contrast to U.S. chemical policies, European Union health officials won't allow new chemicals to enter Europe's marketplace until safety studies have been performed. The **Precautionary Principle** as exercised in the European Union states that *"when an activity raises threats of harm to human health or the environment, precautionary measures should be taken even if some cause & effect relationships are not established scientifically."*

𝔄gain, in contrast, as the Environmental Working Group in the U.S. has observed: **"Even when there is abundant evidence of harm, the {1976} law makes it essentially impossible for the Environmental Protect Agency to ban hazardous chemicals. Instead, EPA has to negotiate slow and incomplete phaseouts, largely on the manufacturer's terms**, which is what happened with

DuPont and 3M. While the Teflon and Scotchgaurd chemicals were slowly being phased out, chemical companies introduced scores of new PFCs. The new chemicals have slightly different molecular structures than the old ones, which makes them less likely to build up in people's blood, but the limited studies that have been done show that they may share many of the same health hazards. Under the outdated U.S. law, the details of these studies—as well as the chemicals' names, the manufacturer, how much is produced and the products they're used in —are often hidden as trade secrets."[5]

Science magazine editor Donald Kennedy issued a strongly worded editorial in a 2007 issue of the magazine about how laws and regulations on toxic chemicals fail consumers: *"The laws and rules regarding the introduction of toxic chemicals into consumer products and the environment are still ineffectual.* ***The U.S. regulatory system for toxic industrial chemicals is not effective and is a threat to public health.*** *"* He urged the U.S. Congress to act and *"stop the chemical industry from continuing to* ***make consumer protection look like a game of whack-a-mole. "***

Agreed officials at the non-profit Toxic Free Foundation, "there are so many hoops for regulators to jump through that is has often rendered them powerless. There are numerous problems with the nearly 40-year-old piece of legislation {Toxic Substances Control Act}. The most concerning is that when it was put in place the TSCA allowed all

---

[5] "Chemicals in Food Wrappers and Outdoor Clothing Linked to Spike in Miscarriages." Bill Walker. Environmental Working Group. May 4, 2015.

62,000 chemicals that were in commerce before 1976, the year it became law, to stay on the market unless the Environmental Protection Agency later found that they posed an 'unreasonable risk'. Furthermore, since the law has been in place, only 5 chemicals have been banned. And while any new chemicals that come to market are required to be reviewed by the EPA, the EPA is only given 90 days to study them. This is of course not nearly enough time to determine the harm they could potentially cause."[6]

 A Frustrating Lack of Transparency

Even when warning labels are mandated by regulations, as with the hazardous chemical formaldehyde, it's only when clothing and other products contain formaldehyde at concentrations greater than 1% that labels are required to warn of possible health hazards. Otherwise, no legal limits exist on formaldehyde content of textiles.[7]

Even more lax regulations apply to nano particles added to clothing. *"No US laws require manufacturers to label clothing that uses either nano-silver or nano-titanium dioxide,"* noted the environmental/consumer group, Green America. How are you expected to detect the possible presence of nano particles that aren't explicitly identified? Advised Green America: *"Watch for labels making claims like 'anti-bacterial', 'odor-eliminating', or 'hygienic', which may indicate the*

---

[6] "The bizarre way the U.S. regulates chemicals." Toxic Free Foundation. March 19, 2015.

[7] "Formaldehyde in Textiles: Technical Bulletin." Cotton Incorporated. 2011.

*presence of nanosilver. Clothing labeled as offering sun protection may
contain nano-titanium dioxide.*"[8]

    Despite an assembly line of synthetic chemicals being added to
clothing during manufacturing, fashion garments in the U.S. aren't sold
to consumers with ingredient labels attached, unlike many other
consumer products such as food. Because there are so many sub-
contractor suppliers along the garment production chain, major fashion
brands often don't know for certain what chemicals are hidden in their
products. That lack of transparency also impedes the efforts of chemical
safety certification services, like Oeko-Tex, tasked with evaluating the
safety of clothing in Europe. How do they keep track for we know they
do not test every garment?

    Being labeled a proprietary secret keeps the identity of many
chemicals in clothing a question mark from even the brand names that
sell the garments. *"It is challenging and often impossible to receive
sufficient and relevant information from suppliers on the chemical
content,"* read a 2022 letter to the European Commission, from a group
of companies seeking ways to incentivize a complete sharing of
information by chemical suppliers.

    Swedish fashion company H&M and the sustainable denim
brand Nudie Jeans were among the coalition of companies signing the
open letter in 2022 to the European Commission demanding more
transparency from chemical suppliers. Specifically, the companies

---

8 "The Trouble with Nanoparticles in Clothing." Green America. www.greenamerica.org

wanted *"more detailed information on the contents of their products in the safety data sheets (SDS) which they are required to provide under the EU's REACH regulations."*[9]

REACH (Registration, Evaluation, Authorisation and Restriction on Chemicals) was initiated by the European Union in 2007, as an agency to enforce regulations requiring chemical companies to register health impacts of chemicals they produce with a central database. But again, it relies on the compliance of companies that may not want the ingredients to be known so who will regulate?

 ## Removing One Toxic Chemical at a Time

A group of 222 scientists from 40 countries published what they called The Madrid Statement, in a 2015 edition of the science journal, *Environmental Health Perspectives*, calling for reduced use of stain and waterproofing chemicals. The entire class of chemicals called PFASs or PFCs "last in the environment for geological time—that is, millions of years—perhaps even longer than humanity," said co-signer Scott Mabury, a professor of environmental chemistry at the University of Toronto. Molecules composing these and other 'forever' chemicals have exceedingly strong bonds between long chains of carbon and fluorine atoms, explaining why they are slow to degrade.

[9] "H&M, Nudie in Call for Chemical Transparency," Ecotextile News, April 22, 2022. www.ecotextile.com

So Why would PFAS ever been created?

Again out of necessity we created fireproofing agents for clothing as women were catching fire from candles with gowns dyed with coal!

The first creation for a fireproof dress was the **Asbestos dress!** They use to spin asbestos yarn that could not be destroyed by fire and even though it is a natural rock it causes **lung scarring** which was discovered in 1900 but not acted upon until 1960! I wonder why! It was being marketed as God's gift to home owners!

Finally, in August 2022, the U.S. EPA finally proposed designating certain PFAS chemicals as hazardous substances. As noted by the Environmental Working Group: *"Today 3M announced that by the end of 2025 it will stop manufacturing the toxic 'forever chemicals' known as PFAS and work to discontinue their use. But it's too little, too late, because 3M has known for more than 50 years that PFAS chemicals are toxic. Global polluter 3M has engaged in decades of deception, knowing its PFAS products were toxic but hiding that information from the public."* This strategy of disinformation is a playbook used by many industries to deceive and misinform the public about other dangers. Continues the EWG: ***"It's why babies in the womb are born pre-polluted with toxic PFAS, and why PFAS exposure is a problem throughout the U.S."***

ʰealth problems linked to PFAS came to wider public attention after Ohio attorney Robert Bilott took on a case in 1998 for a Parkersburg, West Virginia, family, whose cattle were suffering unexplained illnesses. Bilott's work ultimately led to the release of thousands of documents by DuPont, whose Parkersburg plant produced an early type of PFAS known as PFOA. **The documents revealed that DuPont had concealed internal research from as far back as 1961, linking PFOA to negative health effects** and had hidden test results showing PFOA contamination of the local water supply.

DuPont agreed to pay $671 million to settle more than 3,000 personal injury claims in 2017, stemming from the leak of PFOA in Parkersburg; overall, the company has paid more than $1 billion to people affected by this contamination. **Given the range of health impacts linked to exposure to these chemicals—testicular and kidney cancer, organ toxicity, endocrine disruption, reproductive and developmental and immune response---**this seems like a small price to pay.

In early 2018, after settling a PFAS contamination lawsuit against the chemical giant 3M for $850 million, **the Office of the Minnesota Attorney General released documents showing the company also knew about—but concealed or downplayed—the dangers of PFAS for more than 40 years.** 3M, which invented PFOA and used a related compound known as PFOS in its popular Scotchguard fabric product, had conducted scientific studies in the 1970s that documented the chemicals' toxicity, but failed to give that evidence to the EPA.

An investigation by *Time* magazine in 2023, headlined: **"Companies Knew the Dangers of PFAS 'Forever Chemicals'—and Kept Them Secret"**, revealed the findings of a study comparing the **actions of chemical companies hiding the dangers of PFAS to the actions of the tobacco and fossil fuel industries which had engaged in cover-ups. Parallels were striking:** *"PFAS manufacturers suppressing unfavourable research, distorting public disclosure of research that does leak out, withholding information from employees who might be exposed to dangerous levels of PFAS, and not disclosing evidence of PFAS dangers to the Environmental Protection Agency (EPA) as required under the Toxic Substances Control Act...the companies knew the risks associated with the substances they were manufacturing."*

In-house scientists at various PFAS manufacturing plants even stated in company documents written decades earlier: ***"contact with the skin should be strictly avoided."***[10]

Skin contact with PFAS continues to surface as a theme in the testing of clothing products, as we reveal throughout this book. To illustrate a recent example (mentioned in Chapter Three), indicator's of

PFAS's were detected in women's yoga leggings, workout pants, and sports bras during lab testing commissioned by the safety blog, Mamavation, during 2022.[11]

The 32 pairs of yoga leggings and workout pants, and 23 sports bras, yielded chemical indicators of PFAS chemicals and chemical indicators ranging from 284 (ppm) parts per million in LulaRoe leggings, to 58 ppm in Third Love Muse Sports bras, 57 ppm in Adidas Don't Rest Alphaskin Bra, 48 ppm in Champion Freedom Seamless Racerback Sports Bra, 48 ppm in SheFit Sports Bra, to 38 ppm in Nike Women's Medium Support Non-Padded Sports Bra. Among other name brands included in the testing survey were UnderArmour, Lane Bryant, Old Navy.

Most of the chemical exposure from the bras came in the breathable mesh fabric adjacent to the breast and nipples which was made of either polyester or nylon. (You might refer back to the bras and breast cancer section of Chapter Five.) So the clothes these health advocate women are wearing to workout in and sweat in are spreading harmful toxins into their bodies…a bit like smoking while doing yoga!

---

[11] "In Depth: First-of-its kind testing points to dangers and unknowns of PFAS in clothing." Elizabeth Gribkoff. *Environmental Health News*. Feb. 15, 2022. https://www.ehn.org/pfas-clothing-2656587709.html

Obviously, a huge problem exists with finding **PFAS** chemicals in clothing, especially garments you sweat in, because of the history of these substances being documented as health hazards: **able to alter human metabolism, fertility, reduce fetal growth, advance the risk of becoming overweight or obese, and most dangerously, to increase your risk of cancer.**[12]

Environmental Health News reported that *"most of the brands whose clothing tested positive did not respond to multiple requests for comment."* A PFAS science expert, Professor Graham Peaslee of Notre Dame University, told the news service that the paucity of chemical safety regulation of clothing makes it like 'the Wild West' in terms of conduct, with clothing brands often "not even sure what their suppliers are adding" to finished products. As some types of PFAS chemicals are abandoned for use, new ones are developed to take their place and these rarely have been tested, much less proven as safe to health.

 ## A PFAS Link to Military Bases

More than 1,500 drinking water systems nationwide could be contaminated by PFAS, according to a survey by The Environmental Working Group, affecting as many as 110 million people. One of those directly affected, reported Britain's *Guardian* newspaper, has been Mark Favors, living in a rural part of Colorado in an area with water contaminated with PFAS from Peterson Air Force Base. At least a dozen of his relatives have had cancer.

---

[12] "Per-and Polyfluoroalkyl Substance Toxicity and Human Health Review: Current State of Knowledge." Fenton SE. Et al. *Environ Toxicol Chem*. 2012 March.

"*We had four generations that drank contaminated water,*" said Favors. "*We've been there since the 70s only a mile away from Peterson Air Force base and drank well water. We didn't think they'd be dumping an odourless, colourless, toxic chemical into our drinking water that would remain in our bodies for five or 10 years at a minimum.*" The **groundwater well tested** at Peterson Air Force Base had **88,000 ppt** (parts per trillion) of **PFAS**.

At other bases around the U.S., PFAS levels have been detected even higher, in the parts per millions. I would advise everyone near a military base to get their water tested ASAP. *The Military Times* reported that the Pentagon faces a bill of at least 2 billion dollars to clean up the contamination.

This underscores again why **no amount of PFAS should be tolerated. It affects the growth, learning and behaviour of infants and children, lowers a woman's chance of getting pregnant, interferes with the body's natural hormones, alters the immune system and increases the risk of kidney & testicular cancer and thyroid problems,** to name a few. *The Guardian* newspaper in Britain quoted Liz Rosenbaum, who founded the Fountain Valley Clean Water Coalition, as saying: "*It's not a trade-off. You don't get to contaminate our drinking water because we have jobs. A lot of people think the government's going to take care of them. And it's like, they've been killing us!*'

(Here is link to the map of the PFAS contamination in the US. https://www.ewg.org/interactive-maps/pfas_contamination/map/)

Allow me to clarify where most of the most intensive use of PFAS originally came from. The U.S. Department of Defence started using PFAS 50 years ago in the foam used in firefighting. Army uniforms are also coated with PFAS to provide waterproofing, fireproofing, and stain resistance to the clothing. When you leave the army, you give back the uniform which is usually burned in a pit on the base.

Concerning PFAS contamination on U.S. military bases, the U.S. Agency for Toxic Substances and Disease Registry released a massive **852-page toxicology report in 2018**, evaluating 14 of the most common PFAS variants found on military bases and determined that **risk levels to humans** from the **PFAS were 7 to 10 times higher than EPA risk standards**. Special concerns were expressed about how the PFAS—from all sources, not just clothing---persist in the environment, are extremely slow to biodegrade, and act on human and animal life *"in more hazardous {ways} than previously known."* This report prompted the Center for Science and Democracy (of the Union of Concerned Scientists) to demand that the federal government: "ban all new variants of PFAS and new uses for this class of chemicals," and to "add the entire class of PFAS to the EPA's toxic pollutant list and hazardous substance list."[13]

To further clarify, there are over 5,000 types of PFAS, so according to the lab personnel we interviewed in Tennessee for our own PFAS in fabric testing, they only know how to test for 10 of those.

[13] "Fact Sheet: A Toxic Threat." Centre for Science and Democracy.

That's quite revealing because it would be an easy switch for the manufacturers just to get rid of those 10 in their products and replace with some of the lesser known PFAS.

By the time government agencies make PFAS illegal (all of them!) our grandkids will have already been contaminated and their health harmed. That's one reason why I feel a sense of urgency in this book about the need for action.

California's Safer Clothes and Textiles Act made the Golden State the first state to phase PFAS out of clothes and textiles, effective January 2025. But until that time, consumers in California need to stay as vigilant as consumers elsewhere in the nation.

Warned the Environmental Working Group: *"Until it's possible to be certain whether your baby and toddler textile products contain PFAS, your best bet is to avoid anything labeled stain-water- or grease-resistant, or spill-proof, since these are more likely to have detectable levels of total fluorine and higher levels of PFAS. Even products labeled 'green' or 'organic' may contain them."* [14]

When we were in Italy we went to a region contaminated by a manufacturing plant of PFAS called Miteni (former RIMAR) in a town called Trissino. We also shot the dark polluted waters of Cologna Veneta where water testing has been done and high concentrations of PFAS still exist. There is a group there called Moms against PFAS and

---

[14] "New baby textile product tests show concerning levels of toxic 'forever chemicals'". Sydney Evans and Ketura Persellin. Environmental Working Group. November 3, 2022.

we met with the leader who explained to us in detail the effect being exposed to PFAS as a child bearing mother had on her kids first hand. There is a reason why these moms are using their voice! We need to listen!

Ꮒas Anyone Told You About 'Cleavage' Chemicals?

We all need to pay attention to a series of declarations made by the Swedish Chemical Agency, a science research extension of the Swedish government, in a report issued in 2014: One statement was obvious-- **"When textile articles are in direct contact with the skin, substances in the textiles can migrate from the material and penetrate the skin."** And second, not so obvious-- **"Cancer has been associated mainly with exposure to carcinogenic aryl amines which can be formed as a 'cleavage' (a sharp molecular division; a split) product from textile azo dyes."**

Ꮆhis second declaration is really an admission and deserves special attention. A **reductive cleavage**, as referred to in the report, means **when a chemical divides to form ancillary additive substances**, something that the textile industry doesn't like to talk about and a prickly subject that government regulators rarely address.

Ꭺs the Swedish report further concedes about chemical cleavage, *"auxiliary chemicals and unintended degradation products may also be present in the textiles and cause harmful effects on human health and the environment, but these types of substances are not covered by screening study due to the limitations."* **(One obvious limitation being that testing facilities usually don't know what they are searching for when a chemical has cleaved off new toxins.)**

That revelation poses several hide-and-seek challenges for regulators, industry players, and of course, to textile consumers. Under European Union chemical regulation guidelines, REACH, considered among the strictest in the world, the presence of carcinogenic aryl amines formed from azo dyes is banned in consumer articles. But, and it's a huge BUT, *"A majority of the azo dyes of direct application type identified in the current report can form these banned aryl amines by reductive cleavage. Banned aryl amines may still be on the market."*

More than 100 international standards and labels groups exist, allegedly to monitor textile manufacturer compliance with safety regulations, yet according to this Swedish report, **"only about 10 different kinds of textile labelling {exist}that put demands on the textile processing."** In other words, not only do known toxins slip through the monitoring net, so do cleavage toxins slip through, if only because many can't even be identified much less tested for. [15]

Published on: February 9, 2024

Composition claims on clothing labels are often inaccurate

Labels Accuracy Report launches during Fashion Revolution Week 2020

---

[15] "Chemicals in Textiles: Risks to human health and the environment." Report 6/14. Swedish Chemicals Agency. 2014.

European Union Backtracks on Toxin Reform

A copy of the European Commission's 2024 work program indicates the *"EU has abandoned a promise to ban all but the most vital of toxic chemicals used in everyday consumer products."* Also being dropped is a ban on the export of outlawed chemicals from Europe to the rest of the world.

In 2020 the EU had called for phasing out the use of PFAS in the EU because the substances *"can damage the endocrine, immune and reproductive systems"* and the chemicals *"can take thousands of years or longer to degrade."* But as Britain's *The Guardian* newspaper commented, ***"the scope of the bloc's ambition had been weakened in the face of intense industry pressure."*** [16]

What also gets weakened, not only in Europe and the U.S., but throughout the world, is full disclosure printed on garment labelling to indicate the presence of PFAS's in the clothing fibers. As a 2022 science report declared: *"The presence of PFAS ingredients in consumer products, including those used by children and adolescents {the most vulnerable populations} is not typically disclosed to consumers on product labels."* That's generally true for all chemical additives and it's a intentional labelling 'oversight' practiced in most countries.[17]

---

[16] "EU abandons promise to ban toxic chemicals in consumer products." Arthur Neslen. The Guardian. Oct. 16, 2023.

[17] "How Well Do Product Labels Indicate the Presence of PFAS in Consumer Items Rodgers KM. Et al. *Environ Sci. Technol.* 2022.

This entire worldwide fashion industry needs an intervention and a makeover! The industry has known about cancer causing everlasting fluorinated chemicals in our clothing for decades. PFAS were addressed by the government to handle the very slow phasing out process and now the agencies increasingly abandon the commitment, due to "pressure" which, for all we know, could entail threats or bribery from the industry.

How many more have to suffer or die from this harmful poisoning for profit? No company or profit margin is worth one human life. PFAS should be abolished tomorrow, not a week from now, not in a 5-year corporate bull-shit people pleasing plan…but today.

Beware of 'Greenwashers'

Greenwashing is defined as a practice some companies engage in to spread false or misleading statements in an attempt to make products appear friendly to the environment when they aren't. It's an advertising and marketing gimmick, sometimes called 'green sheen', designed to deceive consumers who truly care about the environment and corporate responsibility for protecting our environmental resources. In layman terms no one is really watching, so why not stick some more gold in the pockets. My grandpa always told me, ***"True character is shown when no one is looking."*** As a designer of 22 years in this industry, I can say I have yet to see anyone appear and check labels for the presence of toxins. There is absolutely no meaningful regulation. It is up to the integrity of the designer, fashion house owner, or apparel company to honestly make claims that can be substantiated.

One of my favorite greenwashing brands in my opinion is Reformation. Their motto could be, it looks so good, you just believe it for you want to believe it. But that doesn't make it true. Up-cycled was a term they were using in their marketing early on taking, "unused" or "discarded" fabric and calling it up-cycled. When we (meaning industry folk) go to fabric houses, like my buddy Mike, from the TV show American Pickers says, how much you want for that old thing you're not using? You get a sweet deal and now can call it 'up-cycling' instead of buying new fabric.

But my biggest pet peeve is what the hell does synthetic up-cycled fabric have to do with sustainability? It is still heavily toxic. The styles may look "hippie" but sorry, it's not hemp. My hippie dad would never wear something unnatural as printed rayon or lyocell, for he knows better just by touching the fabric. Yet, the consumer wants that style, that look, for that cheap price point and throw in that its sustainable, and boom, you have a Gen Y online weekend date night sell!

Viscose (semi-synthetic) which by the way is rayon was the first imitation of silk before Nylon discovered when the scientist Hilaire de Chardonnet was playing in a photographic laboratory and stuck his hand in a substance solution made of nitrated cellulose dissolved in ether use to coat glass negatives. Viscose is highly complex to make using a highly toxic carbon bisulphide. The fumes damage the central nervous system, leads to depression, and **impotence!** Later it was linked directly to hardening of the arteries, cerebral vascular disease, stroke and Parkinson's disease. And you wonder why I do not trust these new "tech" fabrications! Dupont being the largest manufacturer according to Fashion Victims spent $250k annually to promote and gloss over the health effects for sexy hosiery and lingerie. They soon called it Rayon and seen as a luxury good triumph of science and industry costing the health of humans.

Environmental 'buzzword' terms like 'natural' or 'eco-friendly' can be used to mislead when placed on labels. *"Even labels that promote a specific benefit, like 'BPA-free,' should be approached with caution,"* observed The Natural Resources Defence Council, exposing greenwashing on its website. *"That's because, as public health advocates note, the chemical industry leans on a laundry list of 'regrettable substitutions,' i.e., similarly toxic chemicals that have become routine replacements for better-known offenders."*

Scientists evaluating the safety of chemicals became some of the first whistle-blowers to issue alerts about greenwashing, one example being Giovanna Luongo, in her 2015 doctoral thesis on chemicals in textiles, who revealed how she tested four garments marketed as toxin-free, but which contained several types of toxins. She wrote: "It is interesting to note that three of the four garments made of '100%

organic cotton' and *branded with 'ecolabels'* contained BT (Benzothiazole), as well as MTBT (2-Methylthio-Benzothiazole), (both compounds used as ultraviolet stabilizers) with concentrations 7 to 30 times higher than the median concentration of the 'ordinary' cotton garments. This suggests that 'eco-labelling' is no guarantee that textiles are free from harmful chemicals."[18]

Ⅽ□ore evidence of deceitful 'eco-labelling' surfaced in 2022, when a report by the Norwegian Consumer Authority cast doubt on sustainability claims by numerous corporate members of the Sustainable Apparel Coalition, a group formed by global apparel industry companies ostensibly to promote planet-friendly goals. Some companies were describing their polyester garments as 'recycled' when in fact, polyester material cannot be reused again. *"Wrong data is worse than no data,"* commented Tonje Drevland, head of the Norwegian Consumer Authority's supervisory department. *"You have to know that what you're saying is correct. You have to have facts supporting what you're saying."* The companies identified as greenwashers in this report didn't have facts or the truth on their side.[19]

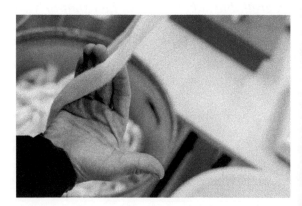

[18] "Chemicals in textiles: A potential source for human exposure and environmental pollution." Giovanna Luongo. Doctoral Thesis. Department of Environmental Science and Analytical Chemistry. Stockholm University. 2015.

[19] "Fashion brands grapple with greenwashing." Lucianne Tonti. *The Guardian* (UK). November 18 2022.

Peeling Back the 'Green Sheen' Curtain

Perhaps the deepest dive into the complexities and confusions arising for consumers about greenwashing deceptions came in a comprehensive 2023 report by Greenpeace, titled "Greenwash Danger Zone." To probe beneath the 'green sheen,' as Greenpeace calls it, scientists for the group examined marketing labels for clothing brands and compared the label claims against tests of the fabrics to identify chemicals and production practices.[20]

Sustainability and eco-friendly claims by 14 clothing brands were examined and compared to fabric and production testing results on garments sold by each company. Among the Greenpeace report findings:

() Despite claims of fabric recycling by the clothing brands, **less than 1% of all clothes were made from old reclaimed textiles**. In addition, only 3% of clothes came from recycled plastics and most of that from plastic drink bottle waste, which shreds into micro-plastics and contributes to global pollution.

() Most of the clothing companies carry garments with **'false certifications'** of eco-friendly compliance. The companies had simply created their own certification programs, rather than using independent third-parties, and then established compliance standards to fit company marketing needs.

() There was a lack of transparency and public information about chemicals added during the chain of production.

---

[20] "Fashion greenwash: how companies are hiding the true environmental costs of fast fashion." Greenpeace.org. April 24, 2023.

() Many of the fashion companies wouldn't even reveal, to Greenpeace or consumers, how many clothes they produce each year to show how much water and electricity and other resources were used in manufacturing.

() Among the clothing brands cited as particularly egregious violators of standards were: *Decathlon Ecoddesign, H&M Conscious, Mango Committed, Primark Cares, Tesco F7F Made Faithfully, and Zara Join Life.*

Concluded the Greenpeace report: *"It is the reliance on polyester for clothing that is fueling the continued growth of fast fashion—and now ultra-fast fashion.* **Polyester is a fundamentally flawed material** *which embodies the devastating impacts of the fossil fuel industry. Greenwashing is a symptom of the bigger disease—the destructive system of the fast fashion business model which can never be sustainable."*

Many Product Certification Agencies Also Greenwash

Periodically clothing manufacturers and fashion brands band together to create certification agencies to set standards for safety, sustainability, and environmental protection, so the companies can point to the certification labels and make claims to consumers designed to appease them to be regular brand buyers. These certifying agencies go by names such as Sustainable Apparel Coalition, Textile Exchange,

Oeko-Tex, ZDHC, Eu Ecolabel, Cradle to Cradle, Higg Index, and

bluesign.

An analysis of more than 100 such certification schemes in

existence during 2022, conducted by the Changing Markets Foundation,

found that these voluntary standards "merely provide a smokescreen for

companies that want to appear to be taking steps towards sustainability"

and accountability to the buying public. Most of the certification

agencies fail to set and enforce strict timelines for companies to comply

with industry goals, such as removing hazardous toxins from fabrics

and reducing the volumes of synthetic clothing.

Transparency for most certifiers is almost non-existent.

Companies that fail to keep promises and meet safety, health and

environmental goals are rarely identified to the public and there is no

evidence of enforcement or consequences from these failures. There is a

lack of independence by the agencies from pressure exerted by

companies that resist playing fairly by the rules. The entire process

seems designed to cushion corporate members from reputational

damage.

Only two certifying agencies—Okeo-Tex and bluesign—were

found to consistently deliver what they promised in holding member

companies accountable to their claims to consumers. Otherwise, most

of the dozens of other clothing certifiers seem engaged in sophisticated

forms of greenwashing by using the certifying agency labels as

camouflage for companies to continue engaging in delays, distractions, and detailing of efforts and goals to bring about positive industry change benefitting consumers.

It's important to point out that even with agencies like Okeo-Tex, they certify fabrics, not the final clothing product. Toxins can still creep into garments through finishing and dyeing processes. This is where confusion sets in for consumers. A certification sticks even though it doesn't belong to the final clothing product, just the original fabric.

For our documentary, I interviewed the technical director for a German testing facility that started the certification agency Oeko-Tex. We independently tested fabrics that had been certified by this agency and we still found toxins the agency failed to identify. They claimed that what we found were 'non-additive' chemicals, such as what results from chemical cleavaging. It was clear to me they had only tested the first in a line of garments before giving certification and not only that, testing was only done on the fabric after it came off the loom, ignoring the processing and dyeing processes where more toxins appear. A lot of money is made off these certification programs that give consumers a false sense of security about the clothes being purchased and worn. I must say the same testing facility when told what to test for in the bra from our documentary did discover 3 x over the legal limit of nonylphenol.If you know what to test, then you can get proper test results but what consumer will know the potential chemical makeup of what they are wearing?

"The fashion industry is one of the least regulated sectors in the world…self-regulation in the form of certification or voluntary initiatives has failed,…It is clear that we are reaching the limit of what can be done without legislation," concluded the Changing Markets report. "This voluntary approach has fundamentally failed to improve performance and to enhance sustainability. Over the last 20 years, while these schemes have proliferated, the fashion industry has become one of the world's most polluting resource-intensive and wasteful sectors. In the midst of a climate emergency, the number one raw material for textile fibre is oil and gas, doubling down the industry's reliance on fossil-fuel extraction."[21]

Backstage LFW 'Let them be Naked' Catwalk

21 "License to Greenwash: How Certification Schemes and Voluntary Initiatives Are Fueling Fossil Fashion." Changing Markets Foundation. www.changingmarkets.org. March 2022.

Binding Policies Needed to Control Microfiber Pollution

"The fashion industry urgently needs to take drastic steps to reduce the amount of micro-plastic fiber shedding from the clothes that they produce. At the same time, far-reaching binding policy measures are vital in tackling microplastic fiber pollution, because only in this way, brands can be held accountable for their contribution to global plastic pollution." –Plastic Soup Foundation, Amsterdam, 2022.

⚜ Keys to Reversing the Cancer Epidemic

"The prohibition of new carcinogenic products, reduction of toxins in use, and right-to-know laws – these are among the legislative proposals which could reverse the cancer epidemic." ---Dr.

Samual J. Epstein, professor of toxicology, University of Illinois.

Chapter VIII: Safeguarding Our Future:

What *You* Can Do, What *We* Can Do Together

 Embrace Quality Over Quantity

"Global fast fashion brands are churning out more clothes than the planet can handle. Today's trends are tomorrow's trash, with our clothes made cheaply and disposed of quickly. It's time to redress the balance, challenge the throwaway mentality and invest in quality over quantity." –Greenpeace.

Vigilance Is the Price of Safety

"We have little to lose, and much to gain, from taking the time to be vigilant about what we put on our skin." –Dr. Samuel J. Epstein, University of Illinois toxicologist, in *Toxic Beauty*, 2009.

Take Inspiration from Wisdom Traditions

An ancient Cherokee philosophy holds that the decisions we make today should result in a sustainable world seven generations into the future. The wisdom of that message should be readily apparent. If only we, as a species, had applied that 'seven generations philosophy' to our handling of toxic chemicals…perhaps, if we were to do that now, there is hope for our future!

New synthetic chemicals are reviewed and approved for consumer uses with no requirement for any toxicity data, beyond first generation effects. Often, such chemicals get approved, with no valid risk assessment data at all, or when independent science does render a safety verdict, that runs counter to corporate interests, too often the people in power, within government and industry, become wilfully deaf to the findings, or they otherwise rationalize away the threats to public health.

It should be clear from reading this handbook, that the *U.S. Toxic Substances Control Act of 1976* is in desperate need of replacement, with a chemicals policy designed to protect and value human health, and the environment, without regard to the current fixation on enhancing industry profits.

What you can initiate, as an individual, to advance a toxins-free agenda consists of a laundry list of attitudes, behaviours, and lifestyle changes.

 ## What *You* Can Do

"We should try to use textile and fabrics which are made from natural fibres and are eco-friendly. Organic clothing should be chosen for the garments which remain closest to the skin most of the time including underwear's, sleepwear and camisoles. We should move in a healthier direction with our right choice of clothing to reduce our chemical load." [1]

"Don't purchase products that are oil-repellant, stain-resistant, waterproof and nonstick, unless you really need them," and, "Support companies committed to phasing out fluorinated chemicals, such as the apparel brands that have joined Greenpeace's Detox campaign."[2]

 ### *Step One is always: Do Not Purchase Synthetic Garments!*

Make a habit of looking for clothing made with these natural fibers (in alphabetical order):

--Abaca (banana fiber)

--Coir (coconut fiber)

--Organic Cotton

--Hemp

--Jute

--Linen

--Peace Silk

--Wool

---

[1] —"Toxicity of Synthetic Fibres & Health". *Advance Research in Textile Engineering*, 2017.

[2] - Dr. Arlene Blum, chemist, and executive director of the Green Science Policy Institute.

If you do still possess synthetics and cannot replace them yet, and you need to wash them, reduce your microfiber footprint by doing the following:

() Wash a full load

() Use toxic-free laundry detergent, such as Seventh Generation, Ecos, (or Borax)

() Use cold water setting on the washer

() Place load on low spin speed

() Use a shorter cycle time

() Use a filter on your washing machine to capture the micro-plastics like from Matter (Gulp) who we interviewed.

() Use a natural fabric softener such as Baking Soda

() Use a front -loading washing machine if possible (they shed fewer fibers than top loaders, according to science studies.)

⚜ Declare Independence from 'Anti's' and 'Poly's'

"People concerned about chemical overloads should be 'anti' any garment that is advertised as being anti-shrink, antibacterial, antimicrobial, antistatic, antiodor, anti-flame, anti-wrinkle, anti-stain, or any of the other 'anti' easy care garment finishes," declared Michael Lackman of 'Lotus Organics'. Additionally, to that advice, stay away from the poly words too, as in, avoid polyester or anything polyvinyl.

--Use unscented laundry products. Even when a cleaner says 'unscented,' there may be fragrance chemicals inside, so the box label should specify 'no fragrance'.

--Instead of using a mechanical dryer, you might try drying your clothes the old fashioned and cheap way---hanging the garments in the sun, on a clothes line.

--Purchase and use secondhand clothing whenever and wherever feasible. Or, for the truly creative and adventurous, design and make your own clothing as a hobby.

--"Reuse is the most environmentally beneficial way of disposing of a garment, compared to recycling, incineration and landfilling."[3]

Exercise consumer choice, endorse sustainability with your buying power. *"Together, we can prioritize purpose over profit and protect this wondrous planet, our only home."* 10-point scale in deciding which garments to design and manufacture and to leave a positive ecological footprint: 1) Is it functional? 2) Is it multifunctional? 3) Is it durable? 4) Does it cause any unnecessary harm? 5) Is it repairable? 6) Does it have aesthetic appeal? 7) Does it fit? 8) Is it easy to care for? 9) Is it globally relevant? 10) Is the product and line simple?

---

[3] "Environmental impact of textile reuse and recycling—A review. Sandin G. Peters G. *Journal of Cleaner Production*. 2018.

Because our bodies release toxins, even during sleep, it's best to sleep naked, to facilitate that release. Make sure your sheets are breathable, made of flax, organic cotton, hemp or un-dyed linen. My personal preference are the hemp sheets I make for all my beds. They do not hold water or sweat, anti-fungal and anti-bacterial naturally and therefore can use longer before washing.

 What *We* Can Do Together

Since PFAS make up thousands of chemicals, one way to reduce exposures is for EPA to regulate PFAS as a class of chemicals, rather than one at a time.[4]

Greenpeace calls on governments to commit to 'zero discharge' of hazardous chemicals ,within one generation, based on the precautionary principle. Using the principle of substitution, safer alternatives need to be innovated with the intention of progressively replacing hazardous chemicals in clothing, and elsewhere, in our lives.

Greenpeace furthermore recommends that regulatory agencies do the following:

() Reduce or ban the use of toxic, persistent or bioaccumulative chemicals in clothing products and their supply chains.

() Reduce or ban the use of non-biodegradable fossil fuel-based materials which shed microplastic fibers.

---

[4] –Tracey J. Woodruff, UCSF professor and director of the Program on Reproductive Health and the Environment.

() Only permit the use of terms such as 'eco' or 'green' or 'natural' if the validity of these label and marketing claims can be verified independently.

() Support the public's right to know with transparency laws that requires companies to reveal all chemical additives and all garment testing and auditing results.

() Phase out synthetic fibers in the production of textiles and require all fabrics sold to be biodegradable and compostable. [5]

 For Governmental Agencies—

1) Recognize the scientific evidence about the rising dangers of microplastic fibers in our bodies and in the environment and institute legally binding measures based on the 'precautionary principle' of harm avoidance.

2) Reduce the volume of synthetic textiles being produced and marketed, using taxation policies if necessary, so that quality can be valued higher than quantity.

3) Establish minimum design requirements for clothing products and set legally binding maximum thresholds for microplastic shedding into the environment.

4) On all clothing and other textile products require information labels for consumers that highlight the documented health and environmental impacts of microfibers contained in the products.

---

[5] "Greenwash Danger Zone." Madeleine Cobbing, Viola Wohlgemuth, Yannick Vicaire. Greenpeace. 2023.

5) Mandate the industrial pre-washing and waste water filtering of textiles to capture microplastics before products are sold to consumers.

6) All washing and drying appliances should be mandated to be equipped with filters sufficient to remove fibers from grey water before entry into public wastewater systems which are no designed to remove fibers.

 For the Fashion Industry---

1)Move away from the 'fast fashion' business model by reducing reliance on synthetic materials and invest in quality clothing products that last longer and don't shed microplastics.

2) Insure that all clothing products are tested for fiber release using independent testing methods and the results are transparent for consumers.

3) Mandate as company policy that all garments produced are pre-washed at least three times before shipping to retailers and sale to consumers.

4) Make a corporate policy effort to extend the life cycle of all products and avoid post-production and post-consumer waste to whatever degree possible.

5) Initiate voluntary information releases to consumers, with labelling, about microplastic fiber release from products, while avoiding making unsubstantiated claims about the recyclability of garments sold.

6) Publicly commit to never engaging in greenwashing, the making of unsubstantiated claims that company products are environmentally friendly when they are not.

Individually, you and I can support companies that signed on to the **'Fashion Industry Charter for Climate Action'** initiated as part of a United Nations initiative in 2018 (and renewed in 2021) with this mission statement: *"To drive the fashion industry to net-zero Greenhouse Gas emissions no later than 2050 in line with keeping global warming below 1.5 degrees."* More than 100 international fashion, clothing and textile companies signed on with individual commitments of meeting goals set in the document, including phasing out coal from the production side of the industry by 2030 at the latest, and adopting 100% of electricity from renewable sources across textile supply chains. Among signatories were Adidas, Burberry, Guess? Inc., Hermes, Ralph Lauren, Stella McCartney, and the Target Corporation. "Fashion Industry Charter for Climate Action."[6] Personally, I want to see all the leaders signing these actions to be wearing plant-based!.

--**Endocrine disrupters have proven their dangers**. These chemicals need to be removed from the marketplace.

--**Publicly shame greenwashing companies**. Call on the U.S. Federal Trade Commission to penalize any clothing manufacturers that make false sustainability claims for their apparel.

---

[6] United Nations Climate Change. https://unfccc.int/climate-action/sectoral-engagement-for-climate-action/fashion-charter

--All garments should carry comprehensive ingredient lists on labels. These would be both primary and secondary chemicals added at every stage of the production process. Total transparency needs to be the consumer standard and a nonnegotiable demand.

--Replace Synthetic Dyes with Innovative Natural Dyes. I have worked on my plant based dyes for 16 years and the sisters I started with started their own company called Stoney Creek Colours in TN which we interviewed in the doc creating powder form plant dyes to use in commercial dying applications. Also, Genetic engineering and fermentation technologies have recently made it possible to obtain natural pigments on a larger scale thanks to dye-producing micro-organisms. Although these dyes are still not widely available, companies such as Colorifix (UK) and Pili (France) are currently optimizing and upscaling production, and the Dutch company Living Colors has recently collaborated with Puma to crease a demonstrator collection using such dyes.

 Support Innovative Sustainability Research

At the only college in North America devoted to the future of textiles—The Wilson College of Textiles at North Carolina University in Raleigh---research and education is constantly being conducted to make the fashion industry more sustainable and to create innovative initiatives to protect the environment.

Among the clever and exciting research projects announced in 2024 were:

--*Structural modification of natural dyes.* Finding strategies to modify natural dyes in textile dyeing to reduce or eliminate the wastewater generated.

--*Accelerating Hemp as a valuable and sustainable domestic textile fiber.* Learning how to process hemp fiber to match textile production requirements and create sustainable processing approaches.

--*Composting unusable textile waste into valuable agricultural resources.* Developing new methods to increase the number and types of materials considered suitable for industrial composting as an alternative to landfill disposal.

--*Converting waste textiles to valuable recyclable fibers and renewable fuel.* Using enzymatic and microbial processes to divert waste textiles from landfills and converting the fibers to biofuel.

--*Efficient removal of textile dyes from wastewater.* Creating polymers that can efficiently remove textile dyes from aquatic systems to reduce environmental contamination and harm to aquatic life.

Ƒold the Fashion Industry Accountable

"If the fashion industry has the power to influence trends, then it also has the power to play a positive role in protecting the planet." –

Greenpeace.

⚜ A few resources:

CHEMACT network is a software platform to manage chemicals of concern without being a chemist.

Seventh Generation is a Vermont company with safe natural fabric softeners made of baking soda & clean liquid laundry detergents.

PlanetCare in 2019 marketed the first external microfiber filter on washing machines in Europe. planetcare.org

Wolf X Rose by Prophetik We are making hemp boxers for men with organic ct./natural rubber waistband & introducing women's

Gulp We interviewed this group in the documentary and they have a microfiber filter also, for washing machines, in the UK.

Xeros developed a filtration technology to remove microfibers from washing machines and wastewater

Where to purchase sustainable denim/jeans:

Able—a goal of minimizing impacts on the environment

Nudie—uses TN natural indigo dye, organic cotton & hemp

Outerknown—from surfer Kelly Slater out of Malibu plant dyed socks (we helped them source) and organic fair trade denim

Triarchy—its environmental impact is disclosed at each stage of the supply chain & moving into TN natural indigo dye with Candiani & they are both friends and passionate for change owned by 3 siblings

Industry of All Nations— natural un-dyed garments, fair trade, also in our documentary, owned by two brothers

(More resources online at **www.letthembenaked.com**)

This Is Just the Beginning

"Using natural fibers whenever possible is a long-term investment in our personal health, in the health of our children, and just as importantly, in the health of our planet. Clothes shouldn't be ecological time bombs. They should be expressions of our desire to live in harmony with our bodies and with the Garden of Eden that is planet Earth, which we were blessed to be born into." -- *Killer Clothes: How Seemingly Innocent Clothing Choice Endanger Your Health*, by Anna Maria and Brian Clement, 2011.

Epilogue: Celebrate the Death of Complacency

"We've been given a warning by science, and a wake-up call by nature; it is up to us now to heed them." ---Bill McKibben

"We are now faced with the fact that tomorrow is today. We are confronted with the fierce urgency of now. In this unfolding conundrum of life and history, there "is" such a thing as being too late. This is no time for apathy or complacency. This is a time for vigorous and positive action."

---Martin Luther King, Jr

⚜ Breaking the Cycle of Dependency

Fast fashion and mindless reflexive purchasing of cheap toxin-laden clothing brands constitute an addiction, a dependency disorder just as insidious and harmful as substance addictions. To be addicted to fast fashion impulse-buying is also to make your body a slave to the toxic chemicals designed to render garments so convenient and affordable.

Experiments using fMRI technology monitored the human brain during buying decisions and produced clear evidence that the pleasure centre of the brain lights up when a desirable object appears, especially if it's on sale and seems like a bargain. This brain response is particularly acute if the purchase involves an item of clothing.[1]

April Lane Benson, a psychologist and the author of *To Buy or Not To Buy: Why We Overshop and How To Stop*, specializes in treating compulsive shopping. She describes the reasons for people constantly browsing products as a form of entertainment. *"I think that it has something to do with the pace that we live our lives at and the paucity of time that so many of us spend in pursuits that really feed our soul. Shopping is a way that we search for ourselves and*

---

[1] "Neural predictors of purchases." Knutson B. Et al. *Neuron*. 2007 January

our place in the world. A lot of people conflate the search for self with the search for stuff."

Identifying this underlying addiction component should be a reason for us to attach even more urgency behind a vision for transforming our bodies and the planet into toxin-free zones. The specter of addiction should be even more of a compelling reason to open our own and other people's minds to inconvenient truths about what we've all too long taken for granted. Allowing fast fashion to thrive means allowing these toxic chemicals to proliferate and thrive. When you put them on your body, what happens? The evidence for harm is overwhelming.

Synthetic chemicals added to our clothing were intended to help make our lives more comfortable and convenient, but the litany of science-backed facts we have detailed tell a more disturbing story. No matter how the clothing industry spins and tries to manipulate us to think everything about their products is okay....***they are not okay.***

Regulators of our fashion industry have applied the end of pipe solutions that attempt to require clothing manufacturers to follow certain protocols. That obviously hasn't worked well. We need a front-end solution that involves identifying the processes of toxin creation and then **reward garment companies to resolve the problems.** The entire incentive structure needs to be changed and a new system put in place because government regulations are so often difficult to enforce or they have been corrupted.

Ƈhis book was written to support the documentary and all the beautiful scientists, researchers, solution inventors, activist, designers, Moms against PFAS, and countless other souls fighting for the cause of safe clothing, good health, and valuing people over profits.

We have to break the addiction cycles of commerce and convenience and champion transparency public policies to protect our loved ones. **Toxins in clothing affects EVERYONE**, unless you spend all your waking hours as a nudist.

You have one body, one life to live, and this opportunity to make a difference for this and future generations.

Ᾱs in my teachings with natural horsemanship, a good test is if the saddle hurts your back, it will hurt the horse…so don't use it. It's the same principle at work with our clothing choices. If your choices hurt you or threatens your child… simply wake up and make healthier choices.

We Need More Heroes, Not Activists

Ƈwo decades ago, I first began talking and writing about hemp and plant-based dyes, when most everyone around me thought this subject was strange and fringy. My hippie dad was one of the few people at that time who supported my point of view and made me feel like I was not the weird one, and that my voice mattered.

When I became a Knight of the Order of St. George, I took an Oath to protect those who cannot protect themselves. So in that spirit consider me on a mission fighting for every person's right to choose safe garments that won't poison their bodies. It's a mission for every one of you who has asked: Where is the industry accountability? Where are the government agencies which should be protecting citizens from harm? Who is checking every product sold to American consumers for harmful toxins that disrupt our health?

No one should be duped and lied to any longer about the 'secret' ingredients used in clothing to provide shortcuts to greater profits. This war for truth and transparency is not political….it's not religious…it is no longer about the validity of the science proving harm. It's over our willful neglect, our complacency, and our reliance on the **synthetic toxic chemical industry that kills innocence and the innocent.**

We demand justice for those we have lost and we demand effective and vigorously enforced regulations for our present and our future kids. Let the Emperors of synthetic toxins be exposed to the truth of the repercussions of their callous actions.

You have a right to choose to buy and wear clothes that don't poison your body. You have a right to not be deceived and lied to about the identity and safety of ingredients in your clothing and other consumer products. You have a right to hold accountable those companies that profit from sacrificing human health. No woman should suffer and die of breast cancer, unknowingly wearing the cause of her suffering. No son should die of prostate cancer from toxic underwear. No daughter should develop pregnancy complications or cervix cancer from endocrine disrupters in her yoga pants. I have lost a mother to Breast Cancer, my hippie dad to cancer, and a child to toxic poisoning which these recent losses have propelled me to walk in purpose to write this book and produce the doc to help save others.

The science research has been done, and the proof has been presented. What remains is for minds to be changed before it's too late, before the bioaccumulations of toxins shamefully injure and kill more good people.

Only by strength in numbers as buyers and voters, only by exercising our collective choices to support sustainability with our buying decisions, can we really hope to establish a toxin free future governed by justice. Share this book and documentary with others. With your help, the dark ages of ignorance will soon to be over and we can proclaim a fashion Renaissance!

'Hippie Dad' Jim & Jeff in his hemp boxers at the Malibu farm

Found this note from my hippie Dad.

Always we Hope

Someone else has the answer

Some other place will be better

Some other time it will all turn out

This is it.

No one else has the answer

No other place will be better

And it has already turned out

At the centre of your well being

You have the answer

You know who you are

And you know what you want

There is no need

To run outside

For better seeing

Not to peer from a window

Rather abide at the centre of your being

For the more you leave it the less you are

Search your heart

And see

The way to do

Is to be

Photo References

Introduction

Figure 1 by Sandrine Lee
Figure 2 Fairlight Hubbarb
Figure 3,4,6 Jake MacPherson
Figure 5 Frank MacDonald
Sketches by Jeff Garner

Chapter1

Figure 1,7,13,14,15,16 © Prophetik
Figure 2 & 3 by Jeff Garner
Figure 4 Courtesy German Archaeological Institute, M. Wagner
Figure 5 by Joseph Nother
Figure 6 Courtesy https://wellcomeimages.org/
Figure 9,10,11,12 by Jake MacPherson

Chapter 2

Figure 1 by Frank MacDonald
Figure 2,5,12 by Jake MacPherson
Figure 3,10 ©Prophetik
Figure 4,8,14 by Joseph Nother
Figure 6 by Sandrine Lee
Figure 7 photo courtesy of H&M Group & Fashion United
Figure 9 by Jeff Garner
Figure 11 Courtesy Kcal News
Figure 13 Courtesy ABC News

Chapter 3

Figure 1,2,3,4,8,9,11,18,19,20,21 ©Prophetik
Figure 5 Courtesy of Jasmin Malik Chia
Figure 6,25 Fairlight Hubbarb
Figure 7 Laurel DePriest
Figure 10 Lillian Liu
Figure 12 Courtesy Science Direct
Figure 13,16,22,24 by Jake MacPherson
Figure 14 Courtesy National Cancer Institute
Figure 15 Courtesy Monica DeCrescentis
Figure 16,22,23 by Jeff Garner
Figure 17 by Olivia Corwin

Chapter 4

Figure 1,3,4,5,6,11 by Joseph Nother
Figure 2,9 by Jake MacPherson
Figure 7 Courtesy of Telegraph
Figure 8 Courtesy of Health Magazine
Figure 10 Courtesy of 5 Gyres

Chapter 5

Figure 1 by Jeff Garner
Figure 2,7,8,9 ,17by Jake MacPherson
Figure 3,4,5,11,12,15 ©Prophetik
Figure 6,10,18 by Fairlight Hubbard
Figure 7 by Angelea Yoder
Figure 13 Courtesy of ABC
Figure 14 by Alexandra Falk
Photo 16 Courtesy of Smithsonian Library

Chapter 6

Figure 1,4,7,8,9 ©Prophetik
Figure 2,3 Sandrine Lee
Figure 5,6 by Jake MacPherson
Figure 10 by Joseph Nother

Chapter 7

Figure 1 by Alexandra Falk
Figure 2,7 by Jake MacPherson
Figure 3,4 ©Prophetik
Figure 6 Courtesy of GreenPeace
Figure 7,8 by Frank MacDonald

Chapter 8

Figure 1 by Lindsey Childs
Figure 2 by Jeff Garner
Figure 3 by Jake MacDonald
Figure 4 by Joseph Nother

Epilogue

Figure 1 by Joseph Nother
Figure 2,3 ©Prophetik
Figure 3 Suzy Demeter

Cover Art by Lilly Piper Faye

Special Thanks

Jim Wilson 'Hippie Dad'
Suzy Amis Cameron
Gerard Butler
Charlie Annenberg
Randall Fitzgerald
Ken Smith
Jenna Hall
Alison Matthews David
Joseph Nother
Madelyn Cunningham
Isabella Garner
Haley Strode
Lilly Piper
Sydney Ross Singer
Don Garner
Kathryn Nelson
Chelsea Brandon
Portia Shaw
Think Films
Amy Shepherd
Darin Olien
Alex von Furstenberg
Oscar Wilde
Lancelot
Ingram

A GLOBAL JOURNEY INTO TOXIC FASHION

Let Them be Naked

FROM EXECUTIVE PRODUCER *Suzy Amis Cameron*

Jeff Garner EMMY AWARD WINNING DESIGNER

INSIDE OUT presents a PROPHETIK and DESIGNSENSORY / POPFIZZ production "LET THEM BE NAKED" directed by JEFF GARNER
EXECUTIVE PRODUCED BY SUZY AMIS CAMERON CO-EXECUTIVE PRODUCED BY JOSEPH NOTHER MADELYN CUNNINGHAM JEFF GARNER
CO-PRODUCERS DARIN OLIEN CARY FLOYD ELISABETH COSTA DE BEAUREGARD CONSULTING PRODUCERS GERARD BUTLER
CHARLES ANNENBERG CONTRIB. PRODUCERS SHARI SANT TRACEY BREGMAN DIR OF PHOTOGRAPHY JACOB MACPHERSON
EDITED BY JORDAN PELTZ FILM SCORE BY WILLIAM WRIGHT
BASED ON THE BOOK BY JEFF GARNER AND RANDALL FITZGERALD